Essential Corfu

by

GERRY CRAWSHAW

Gerry Crawshaw is a highly experienced
travel writer. He writes for numerous
magazines and journals, and has also written
guides to a variety of countries.

AA

Produced by AA Publishing

Written by Gerry Crawshaw
Peace and Quiet section
by Paul Sterry
Original photography
by Martin Trelawny

Reprinted January 1998
Revised second edition January 1995
First published January 1991

Edited, designed and produced by
AA Publishing.
© The Automobile Association 1995.
Maps © The Automobile Association
1995.

Distributed in the United Kingdom
by AA Publishing, Norfolk House,
Priestley Road, Basingstoke,
Hampshire, RG24 9NY.

A CIP catalogue record for this book
is available from the British Library.

ISBN 0 7495 0921 X

The contents of this publication
are believed correct at the time
of printing. Nevertheless, the
publishers cannot be held
responsible for any errors or
omissions or for changes in the
details given in this guide or for
the consequences of any reliance
on the information provided by
the same. Assessments of
attractions, hotels, restaurants
and so forth are based upon the
author's own experience and,
therefore, descriptions given in
this guide necessarily contain an
element of subjective opinion
which may not reflect the
publisher's opinion or dictate a
reader's own experience on
another occasion.
**We have tried to ensure
accuracy in this guide, but
things do change and we would
be grateful if readers would
advise us of any inaccuracies
they may encounter.**

Published by AA Publishing, a
trading name of Automobile
Association Developments
Limited, whose registered office
is Norfolk House, Priestley Road,
Basingstoke, Hampshire, RG24
9NY.
Registered number 1878835.

Colour separation: Mullis Morgan
Ltd, London.

Printed by: Printers Trento, S.R.L.,
Italy

Front cover picture: Vlakhérna

Maps and Plans

This book employs a
simple rating system to
help choose which
places to visit:

 ✓ 'top ten'

◆◆◆ do not miss

◆◆ see if you can

◆ worth seeing if
you have time

INTRODUCTION

Corfu, the northernmost island in the Ionian
Sea and the westernmost part of Greece, is an
enchanting place – thickly covered with olive
groves and cypresses, fringed by sandy
beaches and shingle coves, and well
equipped with hotels, restaurants and tourist
facilities.

Perhaps the best known of all the Greek
Islands, it is particularly popular with the
British, who flock here in their droves in the
summer to soak up the sun on the lovely
beaches and dance the night away at the
countless discotheques which have sprung up
to cater for them. But it would be a mistake to
think that Corfu has been over developed.
The bulk of the touristic development has
taken place within half an hour's drive of the
island's airport, leaving the south and the
north rural while, inland, tourism seems
hardly to have impinged at all on an older way
of life – though for how long things will remain
that way is another matter.

Olive trees are everywhere in Corfu. Some of them are hundreds of years old, and olive oil is a local speciality

Of all the Ionian islands Corfu – Corcyra or Kérkira, as it is known locally – is by far the prettiest and certainly the greenest, even in the hottest months. In springtime especially it is ablaze with broom and blossom of all kinds, but throughout the year, the landscape is covered with greenery, particularly olive trees. Gnarled with age and twisted into fantastic shapes, they cover the 35 miles (56km) from north to south, interrupted by clusters of cypresses.

Lemons and oranges scent the air as they ripen in the sun, and many other kinds of fruit trees grow here, including prickly pears and kumquats – miniature, bitter-sweet oranges, not found anywhere else in Greece; these are preserved and eaten whole, or soaked in syrup. Corfu has its share of vineyards, too, predominantly in the south which, being more flat, has the most agriculture. The grapes are made into wine, mostly for private consumption – the harvest is one of the busiest times in the local calendar.

In spite of the steep growth in tourist traffic in recent years and the changes this has brought about in the economy of the island, the majority of the population is still engaged in agriculture. Cultivated land accounts for almost 65 per cent of the island's total area, and 59 per cent of that is planted with trees. Top of the list are olives, followed by citrus fruits and then other kinds of fruit and nut trees, of which almonds are the most numerous. Just to see the almond trees in blossom in January and February – massed orchards of them, set against a backdrop of the deep blue sea and the silver green of the olive leaves – is a very good reason for coming to Corfu at this quiet and uncrowded time of year.

The island, in fact, enjoys the best of several worlds… beautiful scenery, especially in the northern half, value-for-money restaurants and tavernas offering simple and straightforward local cooking, and a wide range of accommodation from camping sites and clean, simple rooms in local houses to luxury villas, apartments and deluxe hotels. For those looking for sun, sea and sand, Corfu offers numerous beaches. Of its 136 miles (217km) of coastline, the fine expanses of sand along the north and west coasts are

Watersports for the fearless and the cautious can be tried in sheltered bays like Gouvía, on the eastern coast of Corfu

particularly popular with sun lovers, although prone to sudden winds, because the water is usually shallow for a considerable distance and offers safe bathing. Good beaches are limited in and around Corfu Town and Benítsai (Benitses), but other areas with excellent sandy beaches include Glifádha (Glyfada) and Ayios Gordhios on the west coast and Kavos on the east coast in the south. Otherwise, the beaches tend to be shingle or stony and many are small and narrow, though most offer safe bathing. Corfu also has a number of inlets with tiny beaches accessible only by boat.

Many of Corfu's beaches are uncrowded and relatively uncommercialised, but they may be difficult to find being invisible from the road. On the beautiful northeast coast the water becomes deep almost immediately, and offers excellent swimming and snorkelling. Being naturally sheltered, it is very calm and ideal for pottering about in small boats, exploring and discovering, although perhaps not the best choice for those with young children, for whom safe bathing is obviously a priority.

Although tourism has made its mark in Corfu, the islanders – or Corfiots – have hung on steadfastedly to at least some of their old ways and traditions, as can be seen in almost every village. Here, donkeys are still an essential form of transport, and women in local dress can still be seen carrying water and bundles of hay on their heads. Chickens seem to appear from nowhere, and wherever you go you'll see goats and sheep tethered to trees at the side of roads.

The Corfiots themselves are an outgoing, fun-loving and friendly people, and their straightforward charm has been little affected by the increasing sophistication of their environment. The locals have an air of contentment, and understandably so, for Corfu has a special kind of magic that takes possession of visitors and draws them back time and again.

The island's capital Kérkira – better known as Corfu Town – is well worth visiting and exploring. It has a central position on the east coast, with the best-known and most popular resorts located 14 miles (22km) to the north and south. To the north, one of the island's better roads goes to Gouvía and then splits north west to Palaiokastrítsa, probably the most scenic resort on the island. The other road skirts the coastline from Gouvía to Dhasia (Dassia) and Ipsos. At the far end of Órmos Ipsous (Ipsos Bay) is Pyryí, where the road narrows and winds for about 11 miles (18km) to Kassiópi. This stretch provides taxing driving around some tight corners, but offers fine views of many bays below and across the straits to Albania.

On the north coast the only villages of any real note are Ródha (Roda) and Sidhári (Sidari), but the area between Sidhári and Palaiokastrítsa in the north west has some of the best scenery on the island.

The majority of the roads were built during the British protectorate of the islands between 1815 and 1864, and the visitor's first impression is that they haven't improved much since! Lack of government funds results in hasty repairs to the unavoidable potholes which soon reappear. Bad roads often mean bad drivers, but this is not strictly true of the locals, who have to cope with wayward moped- and car-hiring holidaymakers.

Most of the resort areas have expanded rapidly from being small fishing villages, with the result that few have a real focal point. Fishing is still an important way of life, serving the tavernas, restaurants and hotels.

It is hardly surprising that a place so well endowed by nature should have one of the highest population densities in Greece (just under 100,000 people). A slight decline in population during the third quarter of this century has been a fairly general phenomenon: in the case of Corfu it has been chiefly due to the drift away from the rural areas to the large urban centres on the mainland. But the popularity of the island with holidaymakers has helped to stem the flow, and thanks to the Corfiots' inherent ability to welcome visitors and make them feel at home, the island's continuing prosperity seems assured.

From the Old Fortress, the palaçe (centre), Esplanade (left) and other landmarks can be picked out

BACKGROUND

Corfu has been known by a variety of names over the centuries, including Scheria, the name used by Homer. But the one which prevailed – and which is in common local use today – is that of the mythical Corcyra (Kérkira or Kerkyra), whom the sea god Poseidon became enraptured with and brought to the island.

According to archaeologists, the island was inhabited during the Palaeolithic era (70,000–40,000 BC), when it was probably joined to the mainland. The early settlers found an area rich in wildlife, which they hunted for food, and they left evidence of their stay in stone tools found at Sidhári and Límni Koríssia. The earliest Greek settlement on Corfu was probably established in about 775–750BC, and shortly afterwards the island became a Corinthian colony. The settlers constructed a city on the Kanóni peninsula, which, thanks to its strategic setting and the richness and fertility of the soil, rapidly became wealthy and influential. The colonists formed a separate city state second only to Athens, but then suffered from a series of wars and pirate raids. By 229BC Corfu was happy to offer allegiance to the expanding Roman Empire, and was the first Greek city to come under Roman rule. During the ensuing five centuries of Roman authority, the island remained virtually independent, having its own laws and coinage. Many of the forests which covered it were cut down to provide timber for the Roman fleet, thus paving the way for the planting of olive groves which are a familiar feature of the landscape today.

Byzantine Period

When the Roman Empire was divided in two in AD337, Corfu was included in the eastern section, which became the Byzantine Empire. From then on the island was subjected to successive waves of barbarians pouring in from the north. A raid by the Goths was especially destructive, and resulted in the survivors fleeing to a rocky peninsula beyond the ancient city, and this became the nucleus of the old fortress round which the present town has grown. However, the island usually recovered fairly quickly, because of its abundant reserves of wealth. The 11th century saw the beginning of the Byzantine Empire's increasingly desperate attempts to hold on to the island, whose exposed position made it an obvious target for the Normans, Venetians and other nations. The most impressive example of the Byzantine period in Corfu is the church of Saints Jason and Sosipater, in the Corfu Town suburb of Anemómílos. There is also a display of Byzantine art in the Museum of Ancient Art. In 1214, the island was annexed to one of the three independent Greek states which replaced the Byzantine Empire, and better days followed. The fortress of Angelókastro was constructed on the west coast at this time. The Venetians still coveted Corfu though, and finally took over in 1402.

Venetian Period

At that time, Corfu was ruled by a powerful aristocracy for whom it was of crucial importance for their supremacy over the trade routes to the Levant. The Venetians offered the Corfiots security, but in return demanded total

A glimpse of old Venice – the Venetians who once ruled Corfu left many reminders, like this bell tower in Corfu Town

obedience and submission. But the period was not a peaceful one for Corfu. The Genoese raided the island, and the Turks attempted to capture it, first in 1431 and again in 1537 when a 25,000-strong army dealt death and destruction in all corners of the island and captured thousands of Corfiots (who were subsequently sold as slaves), but failed to take the Old Fort. There was another onslaught in 1571, and a final Turkish attempt to capture the island in 1716, when 30,000 Turks landed on the eastern shores, chiefly at Gouvia. But the defences had been well planned by Marshal Schulenberg, an Austrian in the service of Venice, and the Turks were resisted by a 50,000-strong garrison and 3,000 volunteers.

Four weeks of incessant attacks followed, but the defenders finally broke the siege with a victorious sally. A dreadful storm – coupled with the rumour that St Spyridon was threatening the Turkish army with a flaming torch – broke the Turks' morale, and they retreated. In commemoration of this intervention by the saint, a procession is held every year on 11 August in his memory. While there have been olives on Corfu since the Bronze Age it was the Venetians who encouraged the planting of further trees on

Not as old as it looks, the Rotunda commemorates High Commissioner Sir Thomas Maitland, nicknamed 'King Tom'

the island. Every piece of land was put under the olive and by the end of the 17th century there were 2 million trees on the island. The tomato, another basic ingredient in Corfiot cooking was introduced by the Venetians.

French Occupation 1797–1814

During the Napoleonic Wars, Corfu was occupied by the French, the Russians and Turks, and then the French again. The French left their mark most strongly, however; they promoted education, founded a library and set up a printing press (the first in Greece).

British Protectorate 1814–64

After the fall or Napoleon, the Ionian Islands became a British protectorate, under the administration of the Lord High Commissioner, whose headquarters were in Corfu. The first High Commissioner was Thomas Maitland (1816–24), Commander-in-Chief of the British forces in the Mediterranean.

It soon became obvious to the Corfiots that British 'protection' was in fact outright suzerainty. However, despite the Corfiots' misgivings, the British administration brought economic recovery and resulted in the building of a network of roads, a water supply system, and other improvements. At the same time education became more organised, and a new Ionian Academy – the first Greek university – was opened. The British also introduced cricket and ginger beer.

A Part of Greece

The nationalist feelings stimulated by the birth of modern Greece resulted in the Ionian Islands being ceded to Greece in 1864 in return for the election of a British-backed candidate to the Greek throne. But before leaving Corfu the British demolished most of its fortifications, to the understandable annoyance of the local inhabitants.

For the remainder of the 19th century, and up until the start of the tourism boom about 25 years ago, Corfu remained a backwater, which had lost its importance to trade because of the cutting of the Suez Canal and the invention of faster ships. It could not escape the effects of the two World Wars however. The island was used as a base for the British, French and Italian allied forces during World War I, and after the defeat of Serbia, the Serbian government and parliament was transferred to Corfu.

The British have gone but the cricket is as popular as ever – the Esplanade in Corfu Town has been a cricket ground for nearly 200 years

Following the outbreak of war between
Greece and Italy in 1940, Corfu was bombed,
and subsequently occupied by, the Italians,
only to be taken by the Germans in 1943.
These attacks left it in ruins; the library, Ionian
parliament building, theatre and many
churches were destroyed.

Corfu's prosperity in more recent times owes
a great deal to tourism. The islanders were
swift to recognise the benefits this can bring,
with the result that it has an international
airport for holiday flights, and numerous
hotels and other facilities.

CORFU TOWN (KÉRKIRA)

Corfu Town – or Kérkira as it is usually referred to locally – lies on the east coast of the island. It has grown on a projecting bit of land which splits the main town into two sections, Garítsa to the south and Áyios Nikólaos to the north. Right at the tip of the north section stands the town's Venetian fortress, which has been cut off from the land proper by a defensive moat. This is an old town, and throughout the centuries its position has remained little changed. It has evolved rather than being planned, and many of the old cobbled back alleys are accessible to pedestrians only. It is also varied, with reminders of the many different cultures in Corfu's history. There are the wide avenues of the modern sector, and large squares, among them the Venetian Spianada, or Esplanade. Then there are the Neopolitan 'cantounia', leading off the Esplanade: narrow flagstone streets lined with three and four-storey houses built by the Venetians. The Venetian influence throughout the town is strong, but there are also French overtones and suggestions of the English Georgian style. There are also Byzantine churches and fortresses, Venetian steps and monuments, French balconies, and windows with folding shutters. Last but not least the most recent additions to the town are the modern hotels, which provide holidaymakers

Italian-style gardens at the Akhillíon, the summer retreat of a doomed empress

with every amenity. The majority of visitors do not stay in the town itself, however, but come in from the island's many coastal resorts for a day's sightseeing or shopping. Shopping is one of Corfu Town's principal attractions, and visitors can choose between exploring its wealth of historic buildings, museums and monuments, or spending an enjoyable day strolling through the atmospheric narrow streets, bargain hunting or admiring the displays in the many enticing jewellery shops.

WHAT TO SEE

◆◆
AGIA KERKYRA
near entrance of Mon Repos Palace

Agia Kerkyra, or the Church of Palaiopolis, stands on the site of a 5th-century BC temple, in what was the centre of the ancient city, and is the oldest church in existence on the island. Only the outer walls are still standing of the first church here: it was destroyed during the invasions of the 6th century and quickly replaced by a smaller one, which was itself destroyed in the invasions of the 11th century and rebuilt on a still smaller scale. It was renovated once again in 1537 but was badly damaged by bombing in the Second World War. What makes it interesting is that all three churches were built of recycled material from the ancient city, including a 5th-century BC temple and a Roman theatre. An inscription over the west door of the first church states that Jovian, Bishop of Corfu, built it in the 5th century after demolishing the pagan altars which stood on the site.

◆◆◆
AKHILLÍON (ACHILLION) ✓

on the Corfu-Benítsai road, 12 miles (19km) from Corfu Town

The Akhillíon is one of Corfu's most bizarre but most popular tourist attractions. It was built at an altitude of 476 feet (150m) for Elizabeth of Austria in 1890 by the Italian architect Carita, in a pseudo-classical style that many consider the ultimate in bad taste. Kaiser Wilhelm II bought it in 1907 after Elizabeth's assassination by an anarchist in Vienna nine years earlier, and spent his holidays here until the outbreak of World War I. Named after Achilles, Elizabeth's favourite hero, the palace has a modest museum area, comprising a Byzantine-style chapel, a monumental fresco, a Renaissance-style dining room and frescoed columns along the front. The museum also contains a room dedicated to Kaiser Wilhelm, the most popular exhibit in which is the saddle on which Wilhelm sat while writing at his desk.

The park surrounding the building contains numerous copies of ancient statues, such as 'Wounded Achilles', a bronze statue by Herter, a sculptor from Berlin, and 'Achilles Victorious', a bronze statue by Goetz. There are also statues of Muses and busts of Greek poets. Halfway down, in an open pavilion, stands the statue of the empress, her beauty marred by the difficulty of reproducing turn-of-the-century clothes in marble.

It seems strange that a woman as fastidious as the empress apparently was, should have shared the garish taste of the period; but the gardens are well worth seeing.

The palace was completely renovated before being turned into a casino in 1962, but its character has been well preserved.

Open: Visitors can wander in the grounds and visit the museum from 09.00 to 19.00 (Sundays from 09.30 to 14.30); the casino is upstairs. The casino is open from 20.00 to 02.00, and offers roulette, baccarat, chemin de fer and sometimes blackjack. It is only open to non-Greeks, so bring a passport. There is a fee for a single entry or you can obtain a weekly ticket. Men must wear jackets and ties at the casino.

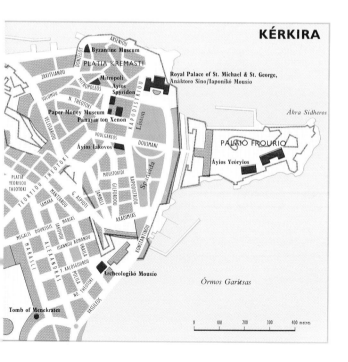

18

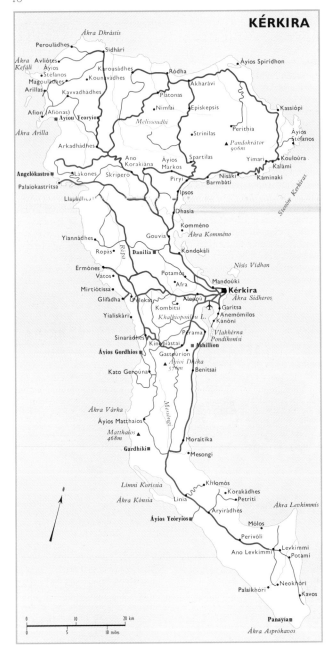

KÉRKIRA

Ákra Dhrástis
Perouládhes
Sidhári
Ákra Avliótes
Kefáli Áyios
Stéfanos
Karousádhes
Ródha
Áyios Spiridhon
Magouládhes
Arillás
Kavvadhádhes
Kounavádhes
Akharávi
Platonas
Afíon (Afiónas)
Nimfai
Episkepsis
Kassiópi
Áyiou Yeóryiou
Melissoúdhi
Ákra Arílla
Strinilas
Perithia
Áyios
Stéfanos
Arkadhádhes
Pandokrátor
906m
Ano
Korakiána
Áyios
Markos
Spartilas
Yimari
Kouloúra
Kalámi
Angelókastro
Lákones
Skripero
Piryi
Nisáki
Barmbáti
Kaminaki
Stenón Kérkiras
Palaiokastrítsa
Liapádhes
Ipsos
Dhasia
Komméno
Yiannádhes
Gouvia
Ákra Komméno
Ropás
Rópa
Danilia
Kondokáli
Nísis Vídhon
Ermónes
Potamós
Vátos
Afra
Mandoúki
Mirtiótissa
Kérkira
Glifádha
Péleka
Alepoú
Ákra Sídheros
Garitsa
Kombitsi
Anemómilos
Yialiskári
Khalkiopoúlou L.
Kanóni
Vlakhérna
Perama
Pondikonisi
Sinarádhes
Kinopiastai
Akhillion
Áyios Gordhios
Gastoúrion
Áyioi Dhéka
576m
Benitsai
Kato Geroúna
Mesongi
Ákra Várka
Áyios Matthaios
Matthaios
468m
Moraïtika
Gardhiki
Mesongi
Limni Korissia
Khlomós
Korakádhes
Ákra Kónsia
Linia
Petriti
Ákra Levkímmis
Aryirádhes
Áyios Yeóryios
Mólos
Perivóli
Ano Levkimmi
Levkimmi
Potami
Neokhóri
Palaikhóri
Kavos
Panayia
0   10   20 km
0   5   10 miles
Ákra Asprókavos

◆◆
ANCIENT CITY
south of town, beyond Anemómilos

The ancient city of Kérkira or Palaiopolis, which is still being excavated, was founded in the 8th century BC just beyond what is now the southern suburb of Anemómilos. At one time the settlement covered much of the peninsula and had two harbours, the southern port of Órmos Garítsas (Garitsa Bay), protected by the city walls, and the Chalikiopoulos Lagoon. It extended as far north as the modern cemetery, as can be seen from the surviving fragment of its walls, which later formed part of a church dedicated to the Blessed Virgin. The most impressive feature is the Tomb of Menekrates, situated in the grounds of a police station at the junction of Marasli and Kyprou Streets in Odos Kyprou, near Garítsa. Discovered in 1843, it is a round structure of roughly-dressed stones with a conical roof, and is thought to date from around 600BC. Close by are the remains of the Temple of Artemis, discovered by accident in the early part of the last century. The gorgon pediment which takes pride of place in the Archaeological Museum is from here. The aqueduct of the ancient city was unearthed at the same time, along with various architectural fragments and pieces of sculpture.

Also of interest are the remains of the western pediment of the Doric temple, discovered in 1911 in the course of excavations. The temple, built in the 6th century BC, had 17 columns along each side and eight at each end, but apart from its massive 80-foot (25m) long altar, practically nothing else has survived.

Finally, excavations have unearthed the remains of a circular monument consisting of six stone columns. This was once crowned by a lion which, like the gorgon pediment, is in the Archaeological Museum.

◆◆◆
ARCHAEOLOGICAL MUSEUM

5 Vraila Street

A few minutes' walk from the Esplanade, this pleasant, modern museum contains a small but interesting collection, ranging from cutlery to fancy jewellery. The most prized exhibit is a 2,500-year-old gorgon pediment, recovered in 1912 from the west face of the Temple of Artemis at the ancient city of Kérkira (Palaiopolis), just south of present-day Corfu Town. It is the oldest known Greek monumental relief, and is well preserved.

The centre of the pediment depicts the hideous gorgon Medusa in flight, with a panther by her side and her two children nearby – Pegasus the flying horse and the hero Chrysaor. According to mythology, Medusa's hair consisted of snakes, and anyone who caught sight of her turned to stone. In the right-hand corner of the pediment is Zeus, sending a thunderbolt

WHAT TO SEE – CORFU TOWN

The gorgon – prize exhibit at the Archaeological Museum

against the Giants, while the left-hand panel shows the young Peopolemos, son of Achilles, killing the Trojan king Priam.

The other showpiece is the Lion of Menekrates that rests on a pedestal in the adjoining room. This sculpture, more than 2,500 years old, is thought to have adorned the tomb of a warrior in the days when Corfu was struggling to win its independence from Corinth. Found on the edge of Corfu Town in 1843, the lion is considered one of the most beautiful ancient animal sculptures known. Also featured is a unique series of statuettes of the goddess Artemis (an important figure of pre-Christian religion), each

depicting her in a different guise – as a huntress, as protector of wild animals and children, and as Artemis of the Hearth. The figures were found in what is thought to have been a workshop making Artemis figures for sale to local worshippers. Other ancient fragments include another gorgon, this one from the late 6th century, and a marble copy of the head of the playwright Menander (342–293BC) as well as vases and fragments of statues.

Open: Tuesday to Saturday, 08.45 to 15.00, Sunday 09.30 to 14.30.
Admission charge.

◆◆

BYZANTINE MUSEUM

off Arseniou Street (the Murayio)
Housed in the church of the Panagia Antivouniotissa (Church of the Virgin Mary) at the further end of the Arseniou promenade to the north of the town, this museum is reached by a flight of steps near the Antranik Restaurant, and contains a comprehensive collection of icons from the 13th to the 17th centuries, mostly from the Venetian era but continuing the Byzantine traditions. The finest are those of the 17th-century painter Emanuel Tzanes, who introduced the Cretan style of church painting to the island. Discovered in 1979 in the abandoned Church of St George below the Old Fortress, they were cleaned and restored and can be seen now in their splendid original colouring.

Open: Tuesday to Sunday, 08.45 to 15.00. Admission charge.

◆
CATHEDRAL

top of Platia Konstantinou

The Cathedral of the Panaghia Spiliotissa (Madonna of the Cave) is an imposing three-aisled basilica. It was built in 1577, and stands at the head of a flight of steps, facing the harbour and the New Fortress. Its greatest treasure is the headless body of St Theodora the Augusta, the island's second saint (after St Spyridon), and the major force behind the restoration of icon worship, whose body was brought from Constantinople at the same time as his. It is held in a silver casket, opened only once a year, to the right of the screen.

◆◆◆
CHURCH OF ÁYIOS SPYRIDON ✓

Odhos Vouthrotou

Located in a small square two blocks back from the Liston and easily recognisable by its red dome, this is the most famous church on the island. It was built in 1589 to replace an older church dedicated to St Spyridon, which was situated in Sarkko and was demolished to make way for the town walls. Experts point out that the bell-tower resembles that of the Greek Orthodox church of St George in Venice, but for most people the most interesting part is inside. Not only does the church contain what is thought to be the greatest weight of silver (in the form of candelabra

and votive offerings) possessed by any Greek church outside the island of Tinos, it also houses the relics of St Spyridon, the island's patron saint. The mummified body is in a chapel to the right of the sanctuary. It is held in an elaborate silver casket, specially made in Vienna; glass insets allow a view of the saint's shrunken head and hands. Slippered feet are exposed for veneration.

A village shepherd on the island of Cyprus, Spyridon became a monk, then a bishop noted for his devoutness and his ability to effect minor miracles. After his death in

Inside the richly ornamented church of Áyios Spyridon

WHAT TO SEE – CORFU TOWN

AD350, a pleasant fragrance is said to have issued from his grave, as a result of which the body was exhumed, found to be undecayed, and was placed in a gold casket. In the 15th century, to save it from Muslim desecration, the body (by this time in its silver casket) was removed to Constantinople.

In 1460 just before the Turkish occupation, Spyridon's remains were smuggled out in a sack of straw strapped to a mule, and taken to Corfu. Four times a year – on Palm Sunday and the following Saturday, on 11 August and again on the first Sunday in November – the casket is paraded through the town to commemorate miraculous deliverances credited to the saint… twice from plague during the 17th century, from a famine in the 16th century, and from the Turks in the 18th century. The church also boasts some Italianate wall paintings which were restored in about 1830. Southeast of St Spyridon's Church is a charming little square flanked by the Church of Panayiaton Xenon (Our Lady of Strangers).

◆◆
CHURCH OF SAINTS JASON AND SOSIPATER

This church stands in the suburb of Anemómilos, and is a beautiful example of 12th-century Byzantine architecture. Built of limestone, brick and tile, it has a flower-filled garden. Place of honour at the entrance to the church goes to two 16th-century icons portraying Jason of Tarsus and Sosipater of Ikonion, the two saints credited with bringing Christianity to the island in the 2nd century. The artist is thought to have been the great Cretan painter Emanuel Tzanes, who worked on Corfu in the late 6th century, and was responsible for many other icons which decorated the church. Inside the entrance is an 11th-century fresco depicting St Arsenios, the 10th-century Bishop of Corfu.

◆
CORFU TOWN HALL
behind the Liston

This low building, decorated with medallions, was built between 1663 and 1691 by the Venetians as an assembly room and was converted into a theatre in 1720. It has been the Town Hall since 1902, when a second storey was added. The outside is adorned with grotesque masks and historical symbols. At one end is a monument to Morosini.

◆◆◆
ESPLANADE ✓

Most visitors to Corfu Town begin by strolling in the Esplanade (or Spianada). Running north to south between the town and the Old Fortress, this great open space is said to be the largest square in Greece. It was once the Venetian parade ground and firing range, but is now a popular place for walking. It was planted with gardens, palms and eucalyptus trees during the Napoleonic

Part 17th-century Venetian, part 20th-century British, the Town Hall was once a theatre

occupation, and is adorned with monuments, including a neo-Classical rotunda in memory of Sir Thomas Maitland, the first Lord High Commissioner; and a statue of Marshal Schulenberg, defender of the island from the Turks. The west side of the Esplanade is lined by the **Liston**, an arcaded terrace containing restaurants, tea rooms and bookshops. The building, which was designed by Mathieu de Lesseps, father of the builder of the Suez Canal, dates from the French Empire period (1804–14) and was inspired by the rue de Rivoli in Paris. Its name comes from the 'list', or 'Libro d'Oro', in which the names of Venetian nobles were inscribed.

At the north end of the square is the Royal Palace, overlooking the half of the Esplanade which now serves as a cricket pitch. The Corfiots were introduced to the game under the British Protectorate, and have played with enthusiasm ever since. There are four local teams which play on Wednesdays, Saturdays and Sundays. The tradition of touring teams, which dates back to the annual visits of the Mediterranean fleet before the Second World War, is now maintained

The Liston, still stylish though no longer exclusive

through the Anglo-Corfiot Cricket Association, founded in 1970.

◆◆
KAPODISTRIAS MUSEUM
near Evropouli
Corfu's least-known museum is situated just out of town, beyond Potames, and is dedicated to the Corfiot John Kapodistrias, first president of the modern Greek state. The museum is housed in the Kapodistrias family residence, a modest Venetian villa set in the midst of a delightfully overgrown garden.
Two rooms contain furniture and paintings, providing an insight into upper-class 19th-century life in Corfu.
Open: Wednesday and Saturday only, 11.00 to 13.00. Admission free.

◆◆
MONASTERY OF PLATITERA
near the northern suburb of Mandoúki
This former monastery is set in a flower-filled, peaceful courtyard. The church itself is small and cool, with much dark panelling and stalls with tip-up 'misericordia' seats more familiar in Catholic and Anglican churches. The ceiling is painted in the Venetian style. There are some rare icons of post-Byzantine art – one, the *Damned and the Blessed*, is regarded as one of the best works of art on the island – and also here are the tombs of the first Governor of Greece, Count John Capodistrias, and of Fotos Tzavellas, one of the heroes and celebrated chieftains of the 1821 Greek War of Independence.
Open: every day 08.00– 19.00. Admission free.

MON REPOS PALACE

on road from Corfu town to Kanóni

The centre of the ancient city used to be here. A Russian general was the first to rediscover the serenity of the wooded promontory and instead of a gun emplacement he built himself a pavilion. Soon afterwards the second British Lord High Commissioner outshone his Russian predecessor by replacing this with the villa of Mon Repos, for his spouse.' Sir Frederick's Folly', as the villa has been dubbed, subsequently passed into the possession of the Greek royal family, and the Duke of Edinburgh, husband of the reigning British monarch, was born there. It is surrounded by a beautiful park. Palace open every day 10.00 to 15.00.

MUNICIPAL ART GALLERY

Odos Akadimias

The newly opened Municipal Art Gallery occupies the ground floor of a renovated building in Odos Akadimias, which leads off the Esplanade. Old maps of Corfu hang in the entrance hall and corridors, while the first room on the right is devoted to portraits of Greek royalty and the next room contains two fine icons from the church of the First Cemetery and a painting of the assassination of President Ioannis Kapodistrias.

Other rooms display works by some of the best-known Corfiot painters, while the final room is devoted to the Baxter Collection, a set of pictures by an English artist and botanist who made a comprehensive study of the flora of Corfu. Among the most attractive of her works are pictures of native wild flowers.

Open: contact the Corfu Town tourist office for opening times.

MUSEUM OF FAR EASTERN ART ✓

Esplanade

This museum occupies the east wing of the Palace of St Michael and St George, and its exhibits include mosaics from the early Christian basilica of Palaiopolis and some 16th-century icons, as well as a collection of Asiatic art. Chinese and Japanese art forms the largest part of the collection, but ceramics, ivory, silk, bronze, stone, lacquer and clay pieces from Korea, Nepal, Tibet and Thailand are also prominent. Of great interest are displays of armour, netsuke, burial figures, plates and screens. The collection was assembled by Gregorios Manos, Greek Ambassador to France and Austria in the early 1900s, whose passion for oriental art led him to buy practically everything he could find at European art auctions. He offered this unique collection of more than 10,000 pieces to the state in 1917, but it was ten years before the government agreed to accept and display it suitably. Manos spent a

fortune accumulating the collection, and died a poor man in 1928. The collection was added to in 1980 when Konstantinos Chiotakis, a Greek merchant from Holland, presented 350 oriental porcelain pieces from the 17th, 18th and 19th centuries. Before that, Ambassador Chadzivasilios, who served in India, Japan and Korea between 1954 and 1970, contributed some Indian sculpture and a display of 16th-century Japanese screens. Rooms left of the grand staircase contain ancient Chinese funerary statuary and bowls, some almost 3,000 years old, as well as pottery and ceramics from half a dozen dynasties. Another room contains intricately designed oriental screens, Thai buddhas, two ancient stone heads, bronzes of dragons and elephants, and hundreds of exotic statuettes. The display of Byzantine art includes many icons, and some frescoes and stone engravings. The statue of Sir Frederick Adams in the front of the face of the palace is by the Corfiot sculptor Pavlos Prosalentis.
Open: Tuesday to Sunday 08.45 to 15.00. Admission charge.

Standing sternly above Mandraki Harbour, the Old Fortress is still in military use

NEW FORTRESS
The New Fortress (Néo Frourio) was built by the Venetians in 1576–89 on a hill dominating the harbour, with massive walls and towers in typical Venetian military style. From the top there is a fine view over the town and the surrounding villages, half hidden in cypresses and olive groves, and of the distant mountains of Epirus and Albania, which seem to merge with the island's highest peak, Mount Pandokrátor. The upper section of the structure was added by the British in 1815. The New Fortress's defences stretch nearly as far as Platia Yeoryiou Theotoki, and the now dry moat houses the

town's fruit and vegetable market; but the building itself is owned by the Greek navy and closed to the public.

◆◆◆
OLD FORTRESS ✓

Cape Sidaro
Built by the Venetians in 1550 on a double peak on the coast, and known as the *Fortezza Vecchia*, it is separated from the mainland by an artificial ditch, the Contrafossa, which is 50 feet (15m) deep and about 100 feet (30m) wide. This artificial island was a suburb of the ancient town, and became the centre of the Byzantine settlement. The Venetians, recognising its strategic importance, transformed it into a fortress, which proved decisive in the successful resistance to Turkish attacks in 1716.

The fortress now serves as a military academy but is open to the public. In the summer months (mid May–September) it is the setting for an exhibition of folk dancing and a sound and light show (English commentary on weekdays only). From the town you cross a bridge to reach the fort, and

WHAT TO SEE – CORFU TOWN

then walk through tunnels past abandoned barracks and along the ramparts to look-out points. The Parthenon-like British Garrison Church, built in 1830, is the single most impressive building of the fortifications. The Venetian clocktower is also eyecatching, its hands stopped forever. You can also walk up to the lighthouse (Castel Nuovo) on the higher of the twin peaks.

The Palace of St Michael and St George houses a stunning Asiatic art museum

At the end of the bridge is the statue of Marshal Schulenburg, who defended the town against the Turks in 1716. *Open*: Public areas 08.00 to 19.00. Admission free; charge for shows.

◆◆◆
PALACE OF ST MICHAEL AND ST GEORGE ✓

Esplanade
Standing on the north side of the Esplanade, the Royal Palace was built by the

English architect Colonel (later General Sir) George Whitmore in 1819 as an official residence for the first British High Commissioner, and as a treasury of the newly created Order of St Michael and St George, which was instigated in 1818 to honour British civil servants who served with distinction in Malta and the Ionian Island Union.

A neo-classical building constructed in Maltese limestone, it has a Doric portico of 32 columns linking two gates (of St Michael and St George) in the form of triumphal arches. Above the cornice are sculptured medallions with the emblems of the seven Ionian islands. When the British departed from Corfu in 1864 the palace became a royal residence for the Greek monarch, but subsequently became neglected and dilapidated. It was Sir Charles Peake, British Ambassador to Athens in the 1950s, who had it restored as a memorial to the British connection.

The State Rooms have been restored to their former glory and now house the Museum of Far Eastern Art. The palace also contains the local offices of the Archaeological Service, the Archives of the island – which contain some important, sadly neglected documents – and the Public Library of 70,000 volumes.
Open: Tuesday to Sunday 08.30 to 15.00. Admission charge – includes entry to Museum of Far Eastern Art.

PAPER MONEY MUSEUM
North Theotoki Street
Claimed to be the only one of its type in the world, this museum is devoted to the bank note in all its shapes and forms. Founded and maintained by the Ionian and Popular Bank it is housed in the stylish upstairs rooms of the Ionian Bank building, which used to be the manager's residence. The building itself was constructed in 1846 and is typical of the style popular during the British protectorate.

In addition to the large display of bank notes, including Greek notes from 1820 to the present day and a rare collection of modern notes from all over the world, the museum also has a well-arranged exhibition showing how a note is designed and produced.
Open: Monday to Saturday 09.00 to 13.00; closed Sunday.

◆
SOLOMOS MUSEUM
Arseniou Street (the Murayio)
Dedicated to the life and work of the poet Dionysios Solomos, this museum is in the house where he lived and where he died in 1857. Solomos introduced poetry to the masses, being the first poet to write in 'demotic' Greek, rather than the complex form hitherto used in literature.

Every Greek knows at least one of Solomos's poems, for he wrote the words which were subsequently set to music and chosen as the Greek national anthem.

The museum contains memorabilia of his life, such as the desk where he wrote, portraits, old maps and photographs, as well as a fragment of manuscript in the poet's own hand.
Open: Monday to Friday, 18.00 to 21.00. Admission free.

Accommodation

Hotel Arion, 5 Emm, Theotoki (tel: 37950). This 105-room 'B' grade hotel is in the Mon Repos area of Corfu Town at the start of the road leading out of Kanóni. Views from the front are limited but there are rear and side views of the pleasant gardens. Facilities include a large swimming pool set in a sun terrace, a poolside bar, barbecue area, table tennis and garden with mini-golf. For entertainment there is frequent live music and a television lounge, and there are a few tavernas nearby. A bus stop for the centre of Corfu Town, two miles away (3km), is outside.

Hotel Cavalieri, 4 Kapodistria (tel: 39336). The Hotel Cavalieri is a 48-room 'A' Grade hotel in the centre of Corfu Town. It doesn't have a swimming pool, but the roof terrace gives good views in all directions. The small dining room serves local and international cuisine.

Hotel Corfou Palace, Dimokratias Avenue (tel: 39485). This 106-room deluxe hotel is close to the centre of Corfu Town, near the old fortress overlooking Garítsa Bay. It boasts a medium-size outdoor pool, indoor pool and a separate children's pool.

Other facilities include sun terraces offering good views and extensive gardens. The public areas are spacious and air-conditioned. The large dining room serves international cuisine, and there are barbecues on the terrace in the summer. Entertainment ranges from cabaret and folk dancing to table tennis, sailing, and card tables. Other facilities include an ice cream parlour, boutique, bookshop and hairdresser's.

Hotel Kerkyra Golf, Alylees (tel: 31785). This 240-room 'A' grade hotel is two miles (3km) north of Corfu Town off the busy coast road. The extensive grounds lead down to the hotel's own narrow sand and shingle beach, and there are well-tended gardens. It is split into two blocks of five and six floors and offers a wide range of amenities, including a large, figure-of-eight swimming pool set in sub-tropical surroundings, a poolside bar, live music, table tennis, electronic games, television and a card room, with tennis, watersports and horse riding available. Breakfast and lunch are buffet-style, while for dinner international and local cuisine are served.

Hotel Marina Beach, Anemómílos (tel: 32783). The Marina is a 102-room 'B' grade hotel by the Mon Repos Lido, two miles (3km) from Corfu Town and close to Kanóni – a somewhat isolated position although there are local shops nearby. The hotel doesn't have a swimming pool, but it does have a small garden, while the

Stay in style near the town centre at the de luxe Corfou Palace

interior is quiet and cool. The restaurant serves local dishes, and there's a pleasant bar/lounge.

Hotel Sunset, Alylees (tel: 31203). The Sunset is a 60-room, modern 'B' grade hotel on a busy main road two miles (3km) north of Corfu Town, just beyond the Kerkira Golf Hotel. It is some distance from a good sandy beach, although there is a small, sandy area for swimming a few minutes' walk away. Hotel features include a large swimming pool with a separate children's section, a poolside bar, sun terraces, and a lounge bar and television. The dining room offers Continental breakfast, and there are poolside snacks, a barbecue and an evening grill room.

Restaurants and Entertainment

Corfu Town offers an excellent choice of restaurants, including several where good regional food can be sampled. Local custom indicates quality. The **Aigli**, in the Liston, the nearby **Akteon**, and the **Rex**, not far away in Kapodistriou Street, all rely heavily on the tourist trade, but at the same time have a regular local clientele, so the food is generally of a high standard. *Sofrito*, the Corfu speciality – meat stewed in garlic sauce and served with mashed potato – features regularly on the menu. Corfu's other contribution to Greek cuisine, *pastitsada* (a tomato stew with pasta) can also be sampled, although it is not as common as it used to be.

The Esplanade (Spianada) is

WHAT TO SEE – CORFU TOWN

one of the most popular spots with visitors, even though restaurants and café prices here are higher than elsewhere in the town. The **Cafeteria Capril**, in the Liston, is good for coffee, ginger beer and snacks such as beefburgers and pizzas.

Two authentic restaurants are **Yisdhakis**, at Solomou 20, off N. Theotoki, and a psistaria at **Ayion Pandon 44**, just off Voulgareos. Others, such as the **Hrissi Kardhia**, on Sevastianou 44, are hidden away in the back streets near Kapodistriou. Menus are almost always prominently displayed, giving you plenty of warning before you sit down. **Quattro Stagioni**, in the old Campiello quarter of Corfu Town, is popular with those who enjoy Italian and Continental cuisine, while a full range of Greek and Continental dishes is served at the **Xenichtis**, in the suburb of Mandoúki, next to the Platitera Monastery.

Many of Corfu Town's hotel restaurants, especially those at the **Corfu Palace**, enjoy excellent reputations, as does that at the casino of the **Achillión Palace**, although the prices at the latter in particular are steep.

The **Venetian Well**, in the back streets of the old town, is a charming restaurant/wine bar serving a variety of European dishes. There is a different menu each night, making it popular for regular visits. If you want excellent seafood, visit the **Argo**, near the port. It's expensive but worth it. Also near the port is the **Cavalier**, where the wall paintings and pianist create a pleasant environment for a steak meal. Of the many bars in Corfu Town, the **Black and White** at the Palace end of the Esplanade and the **Mermaid Tavern** on Aghios Panton Street are among the most popular – and the busiest. There are several discotheques, too, thoughtfully located out of town, about 20 minutes north. The **Playboy** and **La Boom** are among the liveliest.

The narrow streets of Corfu Town have plenty of bars to choose from, but the Mermaid is one of the most popular

RESORTS

AKHARÁVI (ACHARAVI)

Akharávi is a small, relatively undeveloped resort 26 miles (42km) north of Corfu Town. Its main attraction is a huge sand and shingle beach which offers safe bathing. Until recently it consisted of high-quality villas owned by rich city Greeks, but it has been expanded to include many apartments and a few small hotels. To cater for the increase in tourism, three supermarkets have been built together with bars and tavernas, and there are also two discotheques, one with a very good sound system.

Because of the beach, the resort is attracting growing numbers of daytrippers from neighbouring resorts and is losing much of its former quiet charm. It is certainly not as quiet as some holiday brochures like to suggest, but it does have some of the island's best scenery near by. To appreciate this a hire car is practically a 'must'. There are four buses daily to Corfu Town (but one only on Sunday). About half a mile inland lies the tiny village from which the resort took its name, and around the bay is Áyios Spiridhon, with a small, sandy beach, a little lake, and a chapel to Corfu's patron saint. For further variety, the neighbouring resort of Ródha is about 30 minutes' walk away along the beach, while a popular excursion is to the almost deserted village of Períthia, on the northern slopes of Mount Pandokrátor. You can walk up from the village to the summit, which gives a view of the coast of Epiros and Albania, the small islands of Othonoí, Erikoúsa and Mathráki to the northwest of Corfu, the island of Paxoí and distant Keffalonia. The Monastery of Pandokrátor is on the site of a 14th-century monastery. Within the grounds is a well whose clear, fresh water has been praised by many – not least Lawrence Durrell in his book *Prospero's Cell*. Períthia itself is almost hidden in a fertile valley surrounded by barren hillsides. Its winding, cobbled streets, ancient stone-built houses and numerous chapels are a delight. There is even a solitary coffee bar.

Accommodation

Hotel Acharavi Beach (tel: 63460). This is a 60-room, 'B' grade beachside hotel in a quiet spot about five minutes' walk from the centre of Akharávi. Built on two floors, it has front views of hills and rear views of the beach and sea. Facilities include a medium-size pool with poolside bar. The large dining room offers a three-course set menu with waiter service. Entertainment is limited.

Hotel Chrisa (tel: 63104). A 16-room, 'B' grade hotel which opened in 1987, the Chrisa is within 10 minutes' walk of the centre of Acharavi and under 10 minutes from the beach. Built on two floors, it offers front views of mountains and rear views of trees and the countryside. There's no swimming pool, but the hotel does have a sun terrace.

Hotel Ionian Princess (tel: 63110)

A 114-room 'B' grade hotel with character, the Ionian Princess is about five minutes' walk from the beach and the resort centre. It looks like a large, two-storey Greek villa, and has front views of the hills and rear views of gardens and the sea. Facilities include a large sea water swimming pool with children's section, a sun terrace and gardens. There's also a children's playground. The public areas are large and attractive, but the hotel dining room is small and narrow and rather disappointing. For entertainment there is live music and a discotheque in a separate building.

Restaurants

The **Valentino**, on the coastal road, is attractive, with a cool and shady terrace.

◆◆
ARÍLLAS

Situated on the rugged north-west coast of Corfu, Aríllas lies at the end of a winding lane, with a backdrop of hills. It is developing fast, but still has a relaxing, laid-back atmosphere. The village is spread out along a green valley which slopes gently down to the wide sandy bay, fringed by farmland and set between white cliffs on both sides. The beach is long – about half a mile (1km) – and is mainly fine sand with the odd shingle outcrop. It changes character throughout the summer: in the early season

there is not as much sand as there is in July and August, when the water level appears to sink away, revealing a wide stretch of fine sand – the sort that's ideal for sand sculpture! It shelves gently into the crystal-clear sea, making bathing safe even for non-swimmers. Pedaloes, canoes and windsurfers can be hired, and there is also a swimming pool near the seafront where drinks and light snacks can be bought. For basic tourist items there are four gift shops. There are two buses daily into Corfu Town, returning in the afternoon. The journey takes about two hours, as the bus stops in many of the surrounding hill villages, giving the traveller a glimpse of Greek life away from the tourist resorts. The road is winding and narrow and passes through some of the most beautiful countryside in Corfu. The older women of the villages around here still wear the traditional Corfiot costume and invariably have a smile and a wave for their foreign guests.

For a change of scenery, a 45-minute walk along the cliffs will take you to the beautiful bay of Áyios Stéfanos, with its long, wide stretch of sandy beach flanked by small hotels and tavernas. A longer walk, along the cliffs to the south, takes you to Áyiou Yeoryíou, thought by many to be the most beautiful beach on Corfu, while an evening trip to the nearby village of Afiónas, on the headland, gives a spectacular view of the sun

The rocky coast near Aríllas is backed by beautiful countryside

setting over the surrounding countryside, coastline and islands.

Accommodation
Arillas Inn This establishment is on the seafront, across the road from the jetty and the sandy beach. It enjoys a good reputation for its restaurant and café bar, operated by the welcoming Takis and his family. The accommodation is behind, mostly on the first floor, with balconies giving views to the sea. Furnishings are simple but clean and comfortable.

Restaurants
There are at least nine tavernas, three of which are on the seafront. Two, at the top of the village, offer views down the valley to the sea and Gravia island opposite.

◆
ÁYIOS GORDHIOS (AGHIOS GORDIOS)

This west coast resort is about 12 miles (19km) from Corfu Town, and runs alongside a long, sand and shingle beach. It is very quiet, with several villas, a few shops, and some watersports. A hire car is essential, and the drive to Corfu Town via Sinarádhes (Sinarades) is particularly attractive. Alternatively, the local bus runs daily to Corfu Town, but with a limited service on Sundays.

Accommodation

Hotel Aghios Gordios (tel: 53320). This 209-room, 'A' grade hotel stands at the end of the bay, with an impressive backdrop of cliffs in an isolated location near Sinarádhes. The beach is reached down a steep slope off the main village road. The hotel is split into five blocks of four or five storeys, and its rooms have views towards the beach and sea. The small swimming pool is set in a cramped sun terrace, but is surrounded by pleasant gardens. There's a café-style snack bar and a discotheque every night except Wednesdays, often supplemented with live music. The hotel also has a hairdressing salon and other shops.

◆◆
ÁYIOS STÉFANOS (AGHIOS STEFANOS)

There are two places called Áyios Stéfanos: this one is a fishing village-cum-holiday resort on the island's east coast, about 22 miles (36km) from Corfu Town. It is not marked on many maps, but as you make your way down the two miles (3km) of partly asphalted track road winding through the olive groves, you will see one of the island's most enchanting holiday spots – a sleepy, sun-filled cove embraced by green hills, with a cluster of boats bobbing up and down in the bay and whitewashed houses lining the waterfront.

Although the number of visitors increases every year, there is still a timeless air about the place, and the villagers seem to be resisting the temptation to break the spell by modernising the surroundings. There are nevertheless some excellent tavernas, a bar, a well stocked mini-market and a tiny gift shop selling handmade items. A fruit and vegetable van calls every weekday for the benefit of those staying in apartments and villas.

Áyios Stéfanos is the sort of place where parents can relax while children wander safely around, and there's plenty to occupy them – watching the locals leading donkeys or goats, fishermen untangling their catch from the nets, or trying their own hands at fishing off the jetty.

The main attraction is the enormous beach, which has a good selection of watersports. It can become quite crowded with daytrippers from around the island, but there are a number of other unspoilt local beaches well worth a visit, either by walking across the countryside or by taking out a small boat. Kerasia Beach, with its one taverna, is just two bays south of Áyios Stéfanos, and Avlaki is the next bay to the north. There are many other coves and deserted spots in easy reach by boat, and boats can be hired.

Accommodation
Visitors to Áyios Stéfanos have the choice of staying in apartments or very simple, pension-style hotels.

◆◆
ÁYIOS STÉFANOS (SAN STEFANOS)
The other Áyios Stéfanos is a fishing village on the northwest coast of Corfu, along an unmade road leading from Arillas. It has only a limited range of shops, tavernas and one discotheque, but the bustling resort of Sidhári is a 20-minute bus ride away, and a bus runs to Corfu Town twice daily.

The resort is spread around a stretch of sandy beach a mile (1½ km) long, protected by low green hills. At one end of the shallow bay is the small harbour with its caiques, fishermen's houses and beachside tavernas. Further round are villas and apartments, more tavernas, and a few shops selling beach essentials and food.

As time goes by more people are discovering this retreat, but for most of the year it remains uncrowded. Even in the peak holiday months there is more than enough room, because the

Áyios Stéfanos (northwest version)

beach is so long and accommodation in the village still limited. In the high season - and often in the low season, too – all the usual watersports are available, including waterskiing and paragliding. Boat trips are organised according to demand to little islands over the horizon, often with a barbecue, and to Palaiokastrítsa.

A 45-minute walk southwards from the resort along the clifftop leads to Aríllas in the next bay, and a further choice of tavernas. For a change of scene, you can take the local bus to Sidhári, or stay on board and let it take you in and out of the hillside villages and through some of the best scenery on the island, until you reach Corfu Town itself.

Restaurants
In the evenings, the half dozen or so tavernas in the village offer modestly priced Greek dishes and grills, including Corfiot specialities. They take it in turns to lay on Greek dancing and music, so there is always somewhere to go for unsophisticated but enjoyable entertainment.

◆◆
ÁYIOS YEÓRYIOS (AGHIOS GEORGIOS)
This sprawling, purpose-built resort (not to be confused with Áyiou Yeoryíou on the northwest coast) is on Corfu's southwest coast. The two main sandy beaches are among the best on the island, and stretch for over four miles, separated by rocks.

The resort has a scattering of souvenir shops with a limited range of stock, as well as a discotheque and several tavernas dotted about. Watersports include windsurfing, sailing and waterskiing, and an unusual spectator sport is provided in the form of mud wrestling, next to the Florida Cave bar/restaurant, by the beach. Nightlife is limited however; the resort is good for a quiet beach holiday, but is not ideal for young singles and those seeking evening revelry. Popular excursions are to the nearby village of Aryirádhes (Agirades); and to Límni Koríssia (Lake Korission), a huge inland lake surrounded by sand dunes that is becoming a popular picnic spot. Overlooking the lagoon is Mount Matthaíos (Matheos), which offers the energetic a climb to an excellent view.

Accommodation
Hotel Golden Sands (tel: 51225). The Golden Sands is a 62-room, family owned 'B' grade hotel rather off the beaten track but opposite a sand and shingle stretch of beach. Built on three floors with quiet front views of the sea and rear views of the hills and a few villas, its facilities include a medium-size swimming pool, sun terraces, a poolside bar and a large, airy dining room offering buffet breakfasts and three-course menus. Entertainment ranges from live music weekly to regular barbecues.

Restaurants
The **Blue Sea** bar/restaurant is

An unmade road keeps the crowds away from Áyiou Yeoryíou

one of the most popular in the resort, while the nearby **La Perla** shows videos and serves English breakfasts throughout the day.

◆◆
ÁYIOU YEORYÍOU (AGHIOS GEORGEOUS)

Áyiou Yeoryíou is a small, picturesque, 'away-from-it-all' place on the north-west coast of Corfu, with just a handful of tavernas and a couple of small shops. Its appeal lies in the wide, sandy bay – one of the best on the island – offering splendid possibilities for watersports. The only road is unmade, and runs from one end of the bay to the other, with a gap in the middle – apparently because one of the locals refused to sell his tomato patch to the council, with the result that vehicles have to take a two-and-a-half-mile (4km) detour! Dramatically situated at the bottom of steep cliffs, Áyiou Yeoryíou as yet has no local bus service, which means that little development has occurred, even though it's not quite the 'deserted paradise' referred to in some travel companies' brochures. There are no street lamps, so take a torch.

Accommodation
Costas's Golden Beach Hotel (tel: 42380). A two-storey, 62-room 'B' grade hotel which opened in 1986, the Golden Beach is popular with younger holidaymakers and offers a swimming pool, cool public areas and a canopied terrace.

The dining area only serves breakfast, but snacks are available at the bar.

Hotel Aghios Georgeous (tel: 96213) (also known as Aghios Georgious and Hotel San Giorgio). A simply furnished, three-storey, 18-room 'D' grade hotel/pension, in a quiet setting five minutes' uphill walk from the sandy bay. Facilities include a terrace and a small breakfast room/bar.

Barmbáti's white pebble beach, pleasantly cooled by a breeze from mountains behind

Restaurants
Áyiou Yeoryíou does not offer a wide range of restaurants and tavernas, but the **Marina** and the **Nathalie** both offer reliable food, especially fish, as do the **Panorama** and the **Nafiska**.

◆◆
BARMBÁTI
As you go north from Corfu Town, there is a dramatic change in scenery beyond the resorts of Ipsos and Piryi. The road starts to wind upwards on the slopes of Mount Pandokrátor, and then, there

below is Barmbáti, with a long white, shingle beach, contrasting with the silver-green olive trees and deep-blue sea.

On the beach there is a cooling breeze from the mountains behind, and watersports, ranging from waterskiing, windsurfing and parascending, to pedaloes and dinghies for hire. The sheltered waters of this bay make it suitable for children.

In the village there are two supermarkets and a few other small shops selling gifts and handicrafts, while for greater choice both Corfu Town and the resort of Kassiópi are a short bus ride away. There is little nightlife, but this small resort is ideal for a quiet beach holiday.

Accommodation

Hotel Poseidon A modern 64-room hotel, 10 minutes down a winding, steep road to the beach, the Poseidon consists of three small blocks, each three floors high. There's a medium-size swimming pool with sun terraces, a barbecue area and a poolside bar, as well as a small but attractive dining area offering Continental buffet-style breakfasts. The only entertainments are television and table tennis. On a cautionary note, the road leading from the hotel could be dangerous for small children.

Restaurants

Kosta's is one of the best restaurants in the resort. There are several other tavernas scattered about, offering reliable food and occasional Greek dancing.

◆◆◆
BENÍTSAI (BENITSES)

If you are looking for a peaceful break away from it all, Benitsai is not the place for you! If, on the other hand, your idea of holiday bliss is lively bars and discotheques and lots of life and animation, then this resort, about nine miles (14km) south of Corfu Town, could well fit your requirements. In fact, it's *the* most lively, and noisy, resort on Corfu, particularly popular with young British

RESORTS

holidaymakers who have taken over this once sleepy fishing village.

Late nights – and more often sleepless ones – is what Benítsai is all about. The choice of bars is bewildering, while snackbars and tavernas also abound. Discotheques are plentiful too, and all boast the latest sounds.

Benítsai is certainly the most commercialised and 'British' of the island's resorts – in fact, its difficult to find a restaurant specialising in traditional Greek food. That said, it is a colourful place with plenty of shops and bars lining the narrow, busy coastal road. The best hotels tend to be on the outskirts of the resort. Many of the old fishermen's cottages have been attractively converted to shops, tavernas and apartments.

The beaches are narrow and shingly and there is also a sandy, man-made beach, making Benítsai popular with families as well as young people. In the evenings there are plenty of distractions, while Corfu Town is only seven miles (11km) away and can be reached by frequent local buses.

One of the most recently introduced attractions is go-kart racing, and there is a club about a mile (1½ km) from the resort centre. Culture is represented by the ruins of a third-century Roman villa, hidden away behind the main street. Nature lovers will appreciate the emerald valley, lying just behind the village,

an unexpected wilderness criss-crossed by footpaths.

Accommodation

Hotel Achilles (tel: 92425). This modern, 74-room 'B' grade hotel is more than 25 minutes' walk from the centre of the resort, and overlooks its own small, pebble beach, with views from the rear rooms towards the sea. There are sun terraces and gardens. A choice of four-course menus is served.

Hotel Belvedere (tel: 92411). A 180-room 'B' grade hotel which opened in 1987, the Belvedere is built into the hillside on the main coast road between Benítsai and Moraítika. There is a stretch of narrow, shingle beach across the main road and down a steep, narrow, rough track. The swimming pool is rather small for the size of the hotel, although it does have a sun terrace together with a poolside bar. The dining room offers a good choice, including an à la carte menu, and there is a modern bar.

Hotel Le Mirage (formerly Phoenikas) (tel: 92026) La Mirage is a 23-room 'C' grade apartment-style hotel built in 1986, and although in the heart of the resort, lies off the main road in a fairly quiet position. There are several small, narrow shingle strips of beach a few minutes away. Meals are taken at the owner's nearby restaurant.

Hotel Potomaki (tel: 30889). This 140-room 'B' grade hotel is opposite a small, man-made shingle beach right in the heart

Hugely popular Benítsai is a fishing village at heart

of Benítsai, and has sea views. It is popular with British holidaymakers, and offers a three course 'international' menu in a large but disappointingly characterless dining room.
Entertainments include a discotheque, television, table tennis and regular Greek evenings. There are shops virtually on the doorstep, and a nearby bus stop for Corfu Town.

Hotel Regency (tel: 92305). The Regency is a 185-room 'A' grade hotel at least half an hour's walk south of the resort. A subway leads under the coast road to the hotel's own safe shingle beach. There is also a medium-size swimming pool with a sun terrace, set on higher ground behind the hotel and reached by a footbridge from the rooftop. Facilities include a beach bar, poolside bar and children's pool, a discotheque, live music, video, television, table tennis, sauna and massage, card room and

RESORTS

Benítsai has a reputation for non-stop nightlife – the days are for recovering in the sun

writing room, as well as a gift shop and hairdressing salon. **Hotel San Stefano** (tel: 92292). This stylish 250-room 'A' grade hotel stands in a high spot overlooking Benítsai. A brisk 10-minute downhill walk will take you to the busy coast road and beach, and the village is about as far again . Amenities include a seawater swimming pool set in a large sun terrace, a children's pool, gardens, and a children's playground, plus a card room, television, table tennis and tennis. The large dining room gives fine views of the bay and offers buffet breakfasts and an international five-course menu. Live music is a feature in the evenings. The hotel also has its own bookstall, shops and hairdressing salon.

Restaurants and Entertainment

The **Drop-In** bar and restaurant facing the sea has an extensive menu, as does its more stylish but more expensive neighbour **Marabou**. For those who simply cannot survive without at least a weekly helping of roast-beef-and-two-vegetables, **Pat's Place** is the one to visit, while for a taste of local flavour, the souvlakis served at **Costas Bar X** are popular.

One of the most popular discos is **Spiros on the Beach**. Spiros has also opened **Style**, another disco, with good light effects. The **Paradise** has loud music, drinks flow practically all night, and there's an English disc jockey.

◆◆◆
DHASÍA (DASSIA)

The resort of Dhasía lies along a stretch of sand and shingle beach on the east coast of the island, some eight miles (13km) north of Corfu Town. The gently-sloping beaches and shallow waters are backed by dense olive groves, for which this stretch of coast is famous (*Dhasía* meaning forest) and the resort has long been popular for its watersports. Dhasía does not have a central village – instead, most of the resort's shops, restaurants, bars and discotheques fringe the long and busy main road, with others fronting the beach. The beach itself is quite narrow, but many of the hotels have sunbathing areas, often in gardens. Watersports range from waterskiing (there are three separate waterskiing schools on the beach) to paragliding, and there are regular boat trips. Gregory's Boats, for instance, run trips to Kassiópi, Pondikonísi (Mouse Island) and Benítsai.

The two Chandris hotels have tended to dominate the resort, but in more recent times they have been joined by numerous others, as well as small pensions and self-catering developments. There are also plenty of shops and bars. Dhasía is a good base from which to explore the island. Ipsos is only half an hour's walk away, Palaiokastrítsa a 15-minute drive; and there is a good bus service to Corfu Town, eight miles (13km) south, with limited services on Sundays.

Accommodation

Grechotel Daphnila Bay (tel: 35732). This complex consists of a main building and bungalows, set in large grounds, and is popular with those who appreciate virtually non-stop activities and entertainment. There is a steep uphill climb from the narrow, sandy, private beach to the main building. Facilities include a medium-size swimming pool surrounded by a narrow sun terrace with poolside bar and lawns which lead down to the beach with its bar/taverna. The large dining room with covered terrace serves an international menu and buffet breakfast, while snacks are available at the poolside.

The hotel has a busy, lively atmosphere, and coloured beads are used instead of money as internal currency. There is organised entertainment throughout the day and evening, with facilities such as table tennis, electronic games, a pool table, darts, television, 6 floodlit tennis courts, sailing, windsurfing, waterskiing, volleyball, keep fit, chess, board games, discotheque and live music. Children have their own mini-club and playground.

Hotel Amalia (formerly **The Helena**) (tel: 93520). This 26-room 'C' grade hotel is more than 10 minutes from the beach, but compensates with a large swimming pool in a sun terrace, a poolside bar and a friendly, lively atmosphere. It is decorated in Greek style. Facilities include television, records and bar. There's a

RESORTS

small parade of shops and a disco opposite, and a bus stop near by for Corfu Town.

Hotel Corfu Chandris (tel: 97100). Guests of this 301-room 'A' grade hotel can use all the facilities of the Dassia Chandris as well. A few minutes' stroll through the extensive gardens leads to the shingle/sand beach, and the hotel also offers an outdoor seawater pool in a sun terrace, a poolside bar, and spacious, air-conditioned public areas with modern furnishings. An international menu is served, with buffet lunch by the pool. Other facilities include a games room, television, cabaret, live music nightly in high season, tennis and volleyball. Accommodation is in the main hotel building and in small bungalow-style units and villa/apartments in the spacious grounds.

Hotel Dassia Chandris (tel: 97100). The Dassia Chandris is a 251-room 'A' grade hotel facing the shingle/sand beach and shares facilities with its sister hotel, the Corfu Chandris, a short walk away. Amenities include a swimming pool with separate pool for children, tennis, sun terraces, a poolside bar and children's playground. There is live music in high season, a card room, television, table tennis; and watersports are available from the beach. Activities are organised for children. The small dining room offers an international menu. Both the Corfu Chandris and Dassia Chandris run five courtesy buses daily to Corfu Town.

Hotel Elea Beach (tel: 93490). A modern 'A' grade hotel with 210 rooms, the Elea Beach is on

The modern façade of the Corfu Chandris hides a large garden

the beach at the end of a tree-lined avenue. For the hotel's size, the salt water swimming pool and sun terrace are small, but hotel facilities include a poolside bar, and two other bars, live music on Friday evenings, a card room, and electronic games. The large, attractive dining room offers an international menu.

Hotel La Calma (tel: 93755). A 22-room family-owned 'C' grade hotel with character which opened in 1987, the Hotel La Calma is set apart up a steep road leading from the centre of Dhasia and is about 10 minutes from the beach. The hotel boasts a medium-size pool, poolside bar and barbecue, and gardens. Breakfast and snacks are served, and there are tavernas for meals a few minutes down the road.

Hotel Magna Graecia Palace (tel: 93742). Opened in 1985, this four-storey 'A' grade hotel is 10 minutes from the beach opposite the Dassia Chandris. It has character and is superior to many similar category hotels on the island. It offers a large main swimming pool with a separate children's section, a poolside bar, and pleasant gardens. The large dining room offers both international and Greek cuisine, and snacks are also available at the poolside. For entertainment there's tennis, table tennis, electronic games, television and video films, and a bar. A courtesy bus service operates to the centre of Dhasía.

Hotel Paloma Blanca (tel: 93575). A small 36-room 'B' grade hotel in a quiet position on the outskirts of Dhasía, about half a mile from the beach and resort centre. The medium-size pool has a sun terrace and a poolside bar. Poolside snacks are available, and the small dining room offers a four-course set menu. Other amenities include a bar, tennis court and table tennis, and there are themed evenings and organised games.

Hotel Primavera (tel: 91911). A 'C' grade, family-owned hotel with 31 rooms, the Primavera is about 10 minutes from the beach and four minutes from the centre of Dhasía, just off the main road. The hotel's swimming pool is fed from a nearby spring, and other amenities include a barbecue area, poolside bar, gardens, and a children's playground. The small breakfast room serves snacks, and there's a Greek night once a week as well as regular themed evenings.

Hotel San Remo (tel: 93780). A small, 27-room, 'C' grade hotel with character, the San Remo is in between Dhasía and Ipsos, 20 minutes from the beach and up a very steep hill. That said, it is a very friendly hotel, with gardens, swimming pool and poolside bar.

International dishes are served in the dining room and if guests don't like what they see on the menu they are welcome to go into the kitchen and choose their own food. Poolside snacks are also available. Entertainment is limited to the occasional Greek night, television and video films.

Restaurants and Entertainment

The local tavernas have a friendly atmosphere and many of them serve delicious specialities such as fresh-grilled fish, pasta and mouth-watering cakes and pastries. Most of them also organise some sort of entertainment such as live music or dancing. The open-air restaurant of the **Hotel Elea Beach** is right on the beach, and has a good reputation, especially for seafood. Also popular is the taverna belonging to the **Corfu Chandris Hotel**, set in the hotel's extensive grounds. Barbecues are a speciality. One of the most stylish eating/drinking places in the resort is **Malibu**, set in large grounds bordering the beach, and another is **Plantation**, although this suffers from being on the busy and noisy main road. The **Range Bar Pub**, just off the main road, serves a huge range of exotic cocktails, while **Kiss**, an unpretentious beach bar/restaurant, offers the intriguing promise of 'The Best Food You Never Eat'. The **Woodpecker**, **Drunken Duck** and the **Tartaya** are all popular bars, while the discotheques **La Mirage** and **Attalayn** stay open in the small hours.

ERMÓNES

Beautifully situated on the west coast about 10 miles (16km) from Corfu Town, Ermónes has a small beach of shingle and pebbles and flat rocks for

Odysseus may have been washed up on Ermónes beach, where holidaymakers toast in the sun today

sunbathing. A particularly large rock in the bay is said to be a pirate chief turned to stone for trying to steal a sacred icon from the local church.

The beach is overlooked by the Ermones Beach Hotel, from which a funicular railway operates, and the scenery makes a walk to the nearby village of Vátos delightful, although car hire is strongly recommended. Close by, at Ropás Meadow, is the Corfu Golf Club, acclaimed as one of

Accommodation

Hotel Ermones Beach (tel: 94241). This 272-room, Swiss-managed 'A' grade hotel is set apart from the resort. The main building overlooks Ermónes Bay, with a funicular railway down from the hotel to the small beach. Accommodation is in bungalow-type blocks staggered down the cliff face, and the hotel has an Olympic-sized seawater swimming pool with poolside bar. There is plenty of room for sunbathing, or snoozing on the shaded lawn, and children have a playground with a 'jungle gym'. Sports facilities include four tennis courts (two of them floodlit at night), gymnastics, table tennis, archery, a fitness room, diving school, sailing, surfing, water-polo and pedaloes. There is a team of qualified instructors, and equipment can be hired.

The hotel has its own currency exchange, boutique, news stand and hairdresser's, and cars can be hired. For entertainment there is dancing and live music, and a mini-bus goes daily to Corfu Town.

Hotel Athina Ermones Golf (tel: 94226). A 21-room 'C' grade hotel which opened in 1987, the Ermones Golf is within a five-minute walk of a stretch of sandy beach, set in a beautiful bay. The hotel is approached by a very dusty track, but is recommended for families with younger children and those wanting seclusion. All meals are taken at a nearby taverna, and the tennis courts are shared with the Ermones Beach Hotel.

the best courses in the Mediterranean, with a devious stream that meanders across no fewer than 16 of the 18 holes. Clubs can be hired quite cheaply.

According to legend, Ermónes Bay is the place where Odysseus dragged himself ashore after his ship was wrecked, and fell asleep naked, to be awakened to the chatter of maidens, among them the Phaeacian princess Nausicaa. Certainly the bay and the beach where the little river Ermónes leaves the land and plunges down its rocky course to the sea, perfectly fits the description by Homer.

Restaurant

The **Ermones Beach Hotel** has a taverna where one can enjoy choice Greek wines with local specialities and seafood, accompanied by folk music.

◆◆◆
GLIFÁDHA (GLYFADA) ✓

The small resort of Glifádha lies on the west coast, about 11 miles (18km) from Corfu Town, and has one of the best sandy beaches on the island. This is one of Corfu's most scenic resorts, with sandy cliffs tumbling sheer to the beach, to which a twisty but quite good road manages to find a way down.

The beach stretches for about a mile (1½km) and is popular with daytrippers from other parts of the island. A large range of watersports is available, including sailing. Other facilities are limited: there is virtually no nightlife and only a small selection of restaurants, making Glifádha a good choice for those looking for a quiet beach holiday.

In the north of the resort lies the village of Pélekas, which gives good views of the bay, especially at sunset. It was here that Kaiser Wilhelm built a telescope tower so that he could admire the scenery, at the turn of the century. On summer evenings, when he was in residence at the Akhillion Palace, the Kaiser would drive up here to watch the sunset, no doubt aware that, at certain times of the year, the sun appears to slide down the hillside into the sea.

Another excellent beach is accessible from here, and is usually uncrowded. Its disadvantage is that it is reached by a very steep path. Pélekas itself contains a few bars, tavernas and shops. A few miles above Pélekas is Mirtiótissa, yet another fine beach backed by steep, tree-covered cliffs. It's very difficult to reach, but is popular with agile youngsters. Nearby is the Monastery of Mirtiótissa, so called because of an icon of Mary found by a monk in a myrtle bush.

A bus runs from Glifádha to Corfu Town six times a day in the season, and four times daily on Sundays.

Accommodation

Grand Hotel Glyfada Beach (tel: 94201). This 242-room 'A' grade hotel is one of the best on the island, and stands apart on a long stretch of sandy beach. Sumptuously furnished throughout, it has an 'old-world' charm but also offers up-to-date attractions such as a pool and poolside bar. There are two restaurants, and children can take their meals earlier than the adults.

Part of the complex is the Top Sail Club, offering a wide range of amenities from watersports to sunbed hire. It also has a bar, cafeteria, and a gelateria serving home-made cakes and more than 24 different flavours of ice cream. There is a discotheque, and live music most nights; and tennis and watersports are available. The hotel also has a card room, shop and hairdressing salon.

The cliffs at Glifádha – worth driving down for the beach below

Hotel Glyfada Beach (tel: 94257). This modern, family-run 'B' grade hotel with 35 rooms, lies within five minutes of the beach. It doesn't have a swimming pool, but it does have a large front terrace.

Restaurants
The **LM** beach bar/restaurant has a terrace right by the beach, and serves a selection of snack meals.

GOUVÍA ✓

Gouvía is about five miles (8km) north of Corfu Town, and has a safe sand and shingle beach with good views across Komméno Bay. It is popular for family holidays. The centre of the resort (which takes its name from the lagoon on which it stands) is just off the busy main coast road, and contains a sprinkling of small hotels, bars and tavernas. Over the past few years

RESORTS

several new bars have opened up to satisfy young, single holidaymakers. There is a good choice of watersports facilities, including a marina across the sheltered bay.

On the shore are the remains of an 18th-century Venetian arsenal, where ships were once repaired. Although the roof disappeared long ago, and there's not a great deal left to see, the view does make the hike worthwhile. During World War I the bay was used as a naval base by the French fleet. Gouvía also boasts one of the island's most compact little shopping centres, containing a travel office, gift shop, mini-market, jeweller's, boutique

Danilia Village, Gouvía: crafts are sold under the arcades by day, but at night it becomes a major entertainment spot

and leather shop. Another shop specialises in T-shirts, and there is also a restaurant and a rooftop cocktail bar, **Parallels**. For a change of scenery and atmosphere, the bigger resort of Dhasía is nearby. Buses run to Corfu Town five times a day in the season, with limited services on Sundays.

Close to Gouvía is **Danilia Village**, a reconstruction of a Corfiot village as it would have been 200 years ago. Its main street features houses built in traditional Corfu styles, and the Folk Museum has a collection of farming implements and household utensils. There are numerous shops, selling handmade items from carpets to perfumes, and craftsmen can be seen working by traditional methods.

In the evenings the village is transformed into one of Corfu's

most popular nightspots (it usually features in travel companies' excursion itineraries). Typical evenings include international and Greek floorshows with folk dancing, musicians, singers and dancers, together with frequent international cabaret acts. A meal with wine is included in the price of admission.
Open: Monday to Saturday, 10 to 13.00 and 18.00 to midnight. Dinner begins at 20.30 hours. Admission charge.

Accommodation
Hotel Grecotel Corcyra Beach (tel: 30770). This 246-room 'A' grade hotel is just over five minutes' walk from the centre of Gouvia. Set in large grounds leading to its own private beach, it has two blocks of three and five floors, with some accommodation in bungalows. There is a medium-size swimming pool and poolside bar, plus a separate children's pool set in a sun terrace. The gardens are extensive and well kept.
The dining room opening onto the terrace offers an international menu while breakfast and lunch are buffet-style. Tennis, horse riding, and squash are available, as well as watersports, and for children there is a playground and special programme of activities. The hotel has its own discotheque, souvenir shop and hairdressing salon.
Hotel Galaxias (tel: 91220). A 35-room 'C' grade hotel, the Galaxias backs onto the busy main road that skirts Gouvia, but escapes the worst of the

traffic noise. It is about 10 minutes' walk from the beach, and there is a small swimming pool. The restaurant has a good reputation, especially for local dishes. For entertainment there's a discotheque, television and a small bar. Other bars and tavernas are only a few minutes away.
Hotel Louvre (tel: 91506). Although it is classed as 'C' grade, the 25-room family-owned Louvre is recommended to those on a budget for its character and central location, five minutes' walk from the beach. It is a quiet hotel with its own taverna serving good local and international cuisine. Children's menus are available on request.
Hotel Oasis (tel: 91169). A 'C' grade hotel that tends to attract younger holidaymakers, the Oasis has a lively atmosphere, and though situated on the main road, is nevertheless in a fairly quiet area, about 10 minutes' walk from the beach. The medium-size pool has a sun terrace and poolside bar. Disco music is played round the pool nightly, there are organised games, and usually barbecues several times a week. Other amenities include a television and video films.
Hotel Paradissos (tel: 91001). The Paradissos is a 60-room 'B' grade hotel, set on a hill in a quiet part of Gouvia. The narrow shingle beach (about a mile/1½ km away) and the village centre of Gouvia, are down a steep hill and across the busy main road: not ideal for children or those with walking difficulties.

RESORTS

Hotel Park (tel: 91310). This 178-room 'B' grade hotel is about 10 minutes from the beach and the centre of Gouvia, although there are a few shops near by. Features include a large swimming pool with a section for children, a sun terrace and poolside bar, and gardens. The air conditioned dining room serves an international menu. Other facilities include live music weekly, electronic games, television, table tennis, a bar, gift shop and hairdressing salon.

Restaurants and Entertainment
The **Taverna Filippas** enjoys an excellent reputation not only with visitors but with locals, too. Fish is a speciality. The atmospheric and lively **Corfu By Night** nightclub attracts holidaymakers staying in Gouvia itself and revellers from other holiday spots along the coast. Other popular bars and discotheques include **Rumours**, **Whispers** and the **Greedy Monkey**.

◆◆
IPSOS AND PIRYÍ (PYRGI)
The twin resorts of Ipsos and Piryí, about nine miles (15km) north of Corfu Town on the island's east coast, have been dubbed Corfu's 'Golden Mile'. The long, curving bay is easily that length and is bordered by a sand and shingle beach. In the background, the cliffs rise sheer and bare, to culminate in Corfu's highest peak, Mount Pandokrátor. The valley at their foot to the rear of the

Ipsos is part of the 'golden mile' where the music plays all night, but peace is never far away from the lively resort centre

resorts is mainly agricultural, and little tracks lead here and there through olive groves and meadows.

The two resorts appeal to young singles because of their excellent watersports facilities and nightlife. To call Ipsos in high season a lively resort would be a gross understatement!

The small community of Piryí is situated at the end of a long

and straight promenade road, whereas there is no real centre to Ipsos itself, merely a straggly line of hotels, tavernas and shops facing a narrow, stony beach.

This coastal area's situation facing the mainland has made it a favourite target for Turkish raiders over the centuries, and the bay was the scene of major landings in 1537 and 1716. The names Ipsos and Pyryi are said to date from this period. Ipsos means 'height' and local people say that the name was given to encourage the marauding Turks to believe

that the place was difficult to attack. Piryi, meaning 'tower', may refer to towers which were built to give early warning of Turkish raids. As well as the usual watersports facilities, Ipsos also has water chutes, next to Michael's Cocktail Bar, and waterbikes. The bars come in all varieties – disco, video, cocktail, and English-style – and there are tavernas, pizzerias, hamburger take-aways and ice cream parlours. For those staying in self-catering accommodation there is a bakery, butcher's

shop, supermarket and mini-markets, a chemist's and a mobile post office in the peak season. As the sun sinks so the decibels rise, and by early morning Ipsos is alive, with dance floors a mass of gyrating bodies – and so it continues until the sun begins to rise. Small outboard motor boats can be hired for exploring the coast, and water taxis will take you around the bay to Barmbáti beach. Tennis, squash and horse riding are available near by. Piryí offers a small selection of bars, tavernas and shops strung along the approach road. The area is mainly residential and therefore a good choice for those looking for a more relaxing holiday. A pleasant walk can be taken to Áyios Márkos, a picturesque old village with views of Órmous Ipsos (Ipsos Bay). In the 1950s a landslide swept through the village, destroying the majority of the homes. The government granted plots of land to homeless families down on the plain behind Piryí, and even today this area is known as 'New Áyios Márkos. From the old village, with its attractive cottages and cobbled back streets, you can see the new houses laid out on a grid system. Beyond is a view over the bay and some way along the coast.
Áyios Márkos is also worth visiting for its two churches. At the top of the village, 16th-century frescoes almost completely cover the walls of the barrel-vaulted Church of

Pantokrátor, which dates from 1577. In the lower village, the Church of Saint Mercouris is the oldest Byzantine church on Corfu, and contains frescoes dating from the 11th century. Buses run from Ipsos and Piryí into Corfu Town several times a day in the high season, and taxis are usually available on the main road.

Accommodation

Hotel Ypsos Beach (tel: 93232). This 60-room, 'B' grade hotel is in a quiet setting at the end of a short, tree-lined avenue off the busy coast road. It has a medium-size swimming pool set in gardens. The dining room serves an international set menu, and there is regular live music and cabaret. Near by is a good choice of bars and tavernas, and the beach is in easy reach, about five minutes, walk away.
Hotel Platanos (tel: 93240). A 30-room 'C' grade friendly modern hotel in the heart of Ipsos, directly opposite the beach in a small side road.

Restaurants and Entertainment

Parrotts is expensive but enjoys a good reputation for the quality and variety of its fare. Also popular are the **Albatross** and **Zembella's** restaurants. Lively bars include **Michael's Cocktail Bar**, the **Pig and Whistle**, and the **Coach House**. Of the discotheques, the **Albatross** and **Monaco** are probably the best. **Al's Place** serves English-style fish and chips.

◆
KALÁMI

Kalámi lies 19 miles (30km)) northeast of Corfu Town. The British naturalist Gerald Durrell lived locally as a boy before the Second World War, and gives an affectionate and entertaining picture of island life in his book *My Family and Other Animals* (televised by the BBC in the 1980s). Although the area has changed since Durrell's boyhood, it remains a tranquil beach resort, with a small collection of self-catering accommodation, three charming tavernas and a tiny mini-market. The traditional village of Yimari (Guimari), with its bakery and coffee shop, is approximately 20 minutes' walk away.

Kalámi is a good choice for those happy just to soak up the sun and swim from the white pebble beach and flat rocks. A

Kalámi's white pebble beach is increasingly popular

RESORTS

With its cypress trees and little harbour, Kouloúra is one of Corfu's prettiest corners

pleasant walk will take you to Kouloúra, the neighbouring bay, with its natural harbour and small taverna, where you can watch life go by over a leisurely meal. The Durrells reputedly lived here, and it is associated with novelist Lawrence Durrell (Gerald's older brother) while he was writing his book about Corfu, *Prospero's Cell.* There is a bus stop on the main coastal road, about 15 minutes' walk away, but boat or car hire is recommended if you wish to do some exploring. Buses run five times daily to Corfu Town.

◆
KAMINAKI

On the northeast coast of Corfu, where the mountains reach

down to the sea, jagged headlands separate tiny coves and beautiful beaches. Small hamlets are tucked away virtually undiscovered and unspoilt, with romantic names such as Kalámi, Kouloúra and Kaminaki.

Reached by a steep, twisting lane which is hidden from the main coastal road the little village of Kaminaki has few daytrippers, and slumbers undisturbed in the sunshine. Most of the self-catering properties have been converted and modernised from old stone fishermen's cottages, and cling, limpet-like, to the olive- and cypress-clad hillside.

There are now two tavernas in Kaminaki. The one by the beach is owned by a character called Spiriso, and the other is owned by George. The competition is fierce, so whichever taverna you frequent the food will be excellent, and you will soon make friends with the locals and fellow travellers as you sip ouzo and slow down to the Greek way of life. The resort also boasts a supermarket and a gift shop. The crystal-clear water laps a beach of white marble pebbles which is ideal for children and swimmers of a less adventurous kind. Windsurfing and waterskiing are also available here, conditions being ideal for beginners.

◆
KANÓNI
If it wasn't for the closeness of the airport, Kanóni would be a very attractive resort. It has a good range of accommodation and a convenient location only three miles (5km) from Corfu Town. However, some of the hotels are only 300 yards (270m) or so away from the landing and take-off point on the runway, and the whole resort is noisy. On Mondays, when the majority of the flights arrive or depart, most holidaymakers staying in Kanóni tend to go somewhere else for the day! That said, there is no denying that Kanóni has charm. From the shore there is a much-photographed view of two islands lying in the bay – Mouse Island, or Pondikonísi, and Vlakhérna. According to legend, Pondikonísi is the ship which brought Odysseus back from the Trojan wars and which was turned into stone by Poseidon. Pondikonísi has a 13th century church and can be

reached by boat, while Vlakhérna, on which there is a small, white convent, is linked to the mainland by a narrow causeway.
Corfu Town can be reached by local buses which run several times a day, though with a limited service on Sundays.

Accommodation
Hotel Corfu Hilton, Nafsikas Street (tel: 36540). This 273-room deluxe hotel on the Kanóni headland overlooks its own sand and shingle beach, which is a five-minute downhill walk through the trees, and is close to the vantage point overlooking Pondikonísi. The hotel is close to the airport and does suffer from aircraft noise, but less so than many other hotels in Kanóni. Aircraft are heard but not seen from the garden and pool and there are good views to the sea. Facilities are as one would expect of a Hilton hotel, and include a large swimming pool in a garden, with sun terrace and poolside bar. The main restaurant has an international menu, and there's also a poolside restaurant and a grill room. Live music is a regular feature, and other amenities include a health club/sauna, tennis, bowling, watersports from the beach, a bookshop, library, bank, jeweller's and boutique. The hotel also operates its own bus service to Corfu Town.
Hotel Corfu Divani Palace (tel: 38996/7). Situated in the pleasant, residential area of Kanóni, the Divani Palace is an

RESORTS

The tiny island convent of Vlakhérna is linked to Kanóni by a narrow causeway

'A' grade, 165-room hotel with a medium-size swimming pool set in a sun terrace with a discotheque, card room, and a well-stocked souvenir shop.

Restaurants and Entertainment
Mama Linas, opposite the Divani Hotel, and the **Top of the Hill Bistro**, both enjoy good reputations. Among the many bars, **Captain's Wine Bar** is popular.

◆◆
KASSIÓPI
This small fishing village is on the northeastern tip of Corfu, about 22 miles (36km) from Corfu Town. Reached by a winding road that leads around the foot of Mount Pandokrátor, with views over to Albania, it is an attractive, colourful resort, fast gaining popularity with holidaymakers thanks to its backdrop of hills and its pretty coves.

The narrow main street is lined with a wonderful variety of restaurants and bars, handicraft shops, selling locally produced lace and crocheted items, and small mini-markets. It leads to the harbour square, from where the local fishing fleet goes about its work in the age-old way. The brand new white-walled and red-roofed villas which have sprung up everywhere huddle around it and are dominated by the ruins of an ancient castle.

A coastline of rocky coves, stretches of beach and a calm, turquoise sea is backed by a narrow strip of olive groves, rising into the barren land of the Pandokrátor Massif. This is a region of knife-sharp rocks, spiky vegetation, deserted villages, and deep, shady gorges, where sheep and shepherds try to eke a living. The village is strategically set, at the northern approaches to the Corfu Channel and was once much more important. When the Romans took over the island in 227BC, it was a natural stopping place on sea routes, and many famous people are known to have visited it, including the Emperor Nero. During the first centuries of the Byzantine empire Kassiópi was more important than Corfu Town itself. It was raided many times – hence the castle.

Accommodation in Kassiópi is mainly in villas, apartments or village houses. The limited bathing available – there are four beaches, but they're all small – means that Kassiópi would not necessarily be a good choice for couples with children, but the numerous bars and three discotheques give the resort considerable appeal to single holidaymakers.

The beaches around the resort are mainly pebble coves reached by paths around the headlands. Most watersports are available – waterskiing, paragliding, windsurfing, pedaloes and canoes – and there are also boats for hire. A lovely day can be spent exploring the rocky coastline with its numerous tiny bays and coves. The walk to the nearest beach area, which consists of small rocky bays, is delightful – except for the Coke cans and litter thoughtless tourists have dropped. There is a pony-

trekking centre on the edge of the resort.

A local bus service operates to Corfu Town five times a day and once on Sundays: the journey takes about one and a half hours. There is also a daily caique (fishing boat) service to Corfu Town, offering a delightful and unusual way to enjoy the beauty of the island's east coast.

Another attraction is the ruined castle, which was probably built in the 13th century on a much older castle site – and soon destroyed by the Venetians to prevent further rebellion by locals who had refused to submit.

The village church is believed to occupy the site of the Temple of Zeus, visited by Nero (the village name comes from the god Kassios Zeus protector of the far points of a land). It contains an icon known as the Panayi Kassiópi, donated by a painter in thanks for having been saved from a shipwreck. Another icon is that of a blind boy who, in the 16th century, reputedly had his sight restored while sleeping in the church.

Kassiópi is approached by a cliff-edge road which continues on to Kouloúra (see Kalámi), a very pretty little place for a meal.

Other interesting excursions are boat trips along the foot of the cliffs to Nisáki or along the north coast to Áyios Spirídhon. Filippos Boats, at the harbour, offers motor boats and speed boats for hire, and trips are organised by Kassiopi Boats, a few yards away.

RESORTS

Restaurants

The **Taverna 3 Brothers**, right by the harbour, is unpretentious and good value, and specialises in both Turkish cuisine and fresh fish and seafood. The snack bar **Limani** has tables by the sea and lovely views, and magnificent views can also be enjoyed from the restaurant bar **Kastro**, near one of the principal coves.

◆◆
KAVOS

Kavos is a former fishing village, and has developed into a popular, very lively holiday resort, while clinging on to at least a little of its former charm. It is 27 miles (44km) from Corfu Town, which is remote by Corfu standards, but this hasn't deterred the builders, and construction work could prove a nuisance to visitors seeking peace.

The resort's popularity has much to do with the long, wide sandy beach, that stretches for two miles (3km). It is ideal for children and watersports enthusiasts, who can hire a canoe or pedalo, and go waterskiing, windsurfing or paragliding. There are also three-wheel bicycles for hire. Boat trips go from here to the lovely island of Paxoí (Paxos), three hours south, and along the east coast all the way up to Corfu Town and Kassiópi. Most of the accommodation in Kavos is in apartments, with only a couple of hotels of any size, and there is a good choice of value-for-money restaurants and bars, many with bamboo-thatched terraces overlooking the sea. The food, especially seafood, tends to be simply served but plentiful and tasty. There is also a reasonable choice of nightlife, especially at the northern end of the resort, with several bars and no fewer than four discotheques.

Kavos is now one of Corfu's busiest and most popular resorts, but the local people have not stopped milking their goats, making wine and picking olives, although many are now involved in providing local services for the sun worshippers, discotheque-goers and holidaymakers who flock here in the summer months. The approach road has been improved and is of a fairly good standard, though the same cannot be said of many of the narrow roads in Kavos itself. A stroll to the derelict monastery at the very tip of the island is recommended, as are walks through the olive groves to the little-known villages which dot this unspoilt region. A hire car would be useful because of the resort's isolation.

Several buses run daily to Corfu Town.

Accommodation

Hotel Morfeas (tel: 61300). A rooftop restaurant used for barbecues and gala dinners is one of the features of this 46-room 'C' grade hotel, situated about 100 yards (90m) from the sandy beach and within a 10-minute walk of the centre of Kavos. Other amenities include a medium-size pool with diving pool, a sun terrace, television and video films, regular live music and themed evenings for entertainment.

Hotel Panela Beach (tel: 61329). A modern, 21-room 'D' grade hotel, the Panela Beach stands next to the sandy beach in the centre of Kavos. A large sun terrace area leads from the hotel down to the beach, and there is a terrace bar. Apart from regular barbecues, only breakfast is served, either in the bar area or on the sun terrace, but there are plenty of tavernas a few minutes' walk away.

Entertainment facilities include board games, television and watersports such as waterskiing and paragliding.

The big attraction of Kavos is the gently shelving, sandy beach

In conjunction with the local waterski school, the hotel organises a full watersports day which includes tuition and lunch. Greek nights and fancy dress evenings are a regular feature.

Hotel San Marina (tel: 22455). This is a basically furnished and equipped family-owned 54-room 'B' grade hotel on a narrow stretch of sandy beach within a 10-minute walk of the centre of Kavos. It has a small sun terrace, beachside bar, and a dining room offering three-course set menus which include both international and Greek food.

Restaurants and Entertainment

Apart from the hotel restaurants, the **O Naftis** and **Karavas** restaurants enjoy good

RESORTS

reputations, as does **Eve's Garden**, which has a shady terrace and an extensive menu of Greek and international specialities. Popular bars include **Studio 1**, the **Two Georges**, and the **Ship Inn**.

◆
KOMMÉNO

Komméno is an east coast resort set on a horseshoe-shaped bay dotted with yachts and fishing boats. It has three small, sandy, man-made beaches, but otherwise the nearest beach is at Gouvía. Facilities and amenities are limited, making Komméno popular with those looking for a quiet, relaxing holiday, but the resorts of Gouvía and Dhasía are close enough for shopping and nightlife. Corfu Town lies approximately seven miles (11km) away. Komméno Bay itself is a heavily wooded inlet whose forested hills provide a good view out to sea.

Accommodation

Grehotel Corfu Imperial (tel: 39052) (formerly the Hotel Astir Palace). This 308-room deluxe hotel has undergone major refurbishment and is one of the best on the island. It occupies an isolated position on its own headland, with two private small, sandy, man-made beaches within a few minutes' walk. There are good views from the front of the hotel towards the sea. The large seawater swimming pool is set in a sun terrace, with a poolside bar and gardens leading down to the beach. Facilities include a large air-conditioned restaurant and an

Rich, sub-tropical growth helps to hide the development of the coast around Kondokáli

open-air taverna, a nightclub, cardroom, and facilities for table tennis, tennis, and watersports. The hotel has its own gift shop, boutique and hairdressing salon. Because of the hotel's location, car hire is strongly recommended.
Hotel Radovas (tel: 91218). This 115-room 'A' grade hotel complex occupies a quiet position about five minutes' walk from the waterfront at

Komméno Bay, and has a large swimming pool with a section for children, sun terrace surrounded by Astro turf, a poolside bar, and gardens. For entertainment there's television, video, tennis, electronic games, a regular discotheque, and occasional Greek evenings. There's also a souvenir shop and hairdressing salon in the hotel.

Restaurant
The **Mimose Restaurant** is popular for a meal or a drink in the evenings.

◆◆
KONDOKÁLI (KONTOKALI)
A colourful resort lying south of Gouvía on the island's east coast, about five miles (8km) from Corfu Town, Kondokáli has shops and tavernas running for some distance on both sides of a narrow road, to which the main coastal road lies parallel.
It is on a lagoon which was once a Venetian harbour, and is now a marina attracting private yachts from all over Europe. A tourist office has been opened for those who

RESORTS

arrive by yacht as well as for hotel residents.

The village is set back off the main road, with side roads leading to pebble beaches where there are plenty of watersports to try out. For lunch and dinner there are many traditional tavernas. The name Kondokáli originated with a local seafarer called Christophoros Kontokali who successfully captured a war vessel at the Battle of Lepanto in 1571. His reward for the capture was a grant of land on the peninsula, on which the ruins of his house can still be seen.

A local bus runs daily to Corfu Town, with limited services on Sundays.

Luxury sun-lounging at the Kontokali Palace

Accommodation

Hotel Konotokali Bay (tel: 38736). This 237-room deluxe hotel is a 15-minute walk from the resort centre, and stands on a peninsula overlooking two man-made beaches and a small marina. It offers a large salt-water swimming pool set in a sun terrace, with a poolside bar and small gardens. The interior is somewhat dull, but entertainment facilities include a discotheque/nightclub, table tennis, electronic games, and a tennis court. The hotel also has its own shops and hairdresser.

Restaurants

The **Pipilas** has been going strong since 1924, and is noted for its traditional Greek food, and fish and seafood specialities. Two other popular

restaurants in Kondokáli are the **Fish Taverna** and the **Cozy**, while the help-yourself buffet brunches at the **Cottage Inn** – which also offers more than 50 different cocktails – are much in demand.

MALTAS ST BARBARA

Those who came across Maltas several years ago could scarcely believe their good fortune, for its long, perfect sandy beach usually had scarcely anybody on it. It seemed too good to be true. Corfu Town was only an hour's drive away, and yet there were no crowds, souvenir shops, developments or hotels. Instead, there were merely three tavernas on the magnificent beach patiently waiting for customers. There was no snag – merely that Maltas was largely undiscovered!

Now, several years later, Maltas *has* changed, but only slightly. Sunbeds and umbrellas can now be hired, as can some rather elderly mopeds, and there are even watersports in the peak summer months.

The Santa Barbara Taverna has expanded its menu to include pepper steak, tuna fish salad and omelettes in addition to the normal Greek fare, and often has entertainment of sorts, usually Greek dancing. And they're still promising a telephone! Essentially, Maltas remains much as it was years ago – a simple resort, offering simple pleasures. It lies just south of Áyios Yeóryios.

MESONGÍ (MESSONGI)

Mesongí is an attractive little resort on the east coast of Corfu, at the end of a narrow lane leading from the main coastal road. Three good hotels form part of the small town square, but otherwise the resort has very limited shopping facilities or nightlife. The long and narrow shingle beach is safe for non-swimmers and attracts families with children, as well as young people, but although an increasing amount of development is taking place, the resort remains relatively quiet. There are good mountain walks nearby. Adjacent to Mesongí is Moraítika, where the large Mesongí Beach Hotel is located (see Moraítika), and the hotel provides most of the entertainment.

Interesting excursions can be made to Mount Matthaíos (Matheos) and the Limni Koríssia, and buses run several times a day to Corfu Town, 14 miles (24km) to the north, with limited services on Sundays.

Accommodation

Hotel Gemini (tel: 55398). The Gemini is a basically furnished and equipped 60-room 'B' grade hotel forming part of the village square in Mesongí, close to the hotels **Rossis** and **Melissa Beach**. The beach is a minute away, and there is a swimming pool in a small sun terrace, with, for entertainment, a little restaurant, television, electronic games, and a bar.

The twin resorts of Mesongí and Moraítika have good walking country near by

Restaurants and Entertainment

The **Galini** has a terrace by the water's edge and a good reputation. The **Messonghi Pub** and the **Gemini Bar** are both popular, as are the discotheques **Scorpion**, **Flamingos** and the **Limbo**.

♦♦
MORAÍTIKA

The village of Moraitika nestles on a hillside about 13 miles (20km) south of Corfu Town and comprises a small number of tavernas and shops on either side of the main coastal road. The safe sand and shingle beach is a 10-minute walk away, and offers a good choice of watersports.

In the evenings, most visitors gravitate to the Messonghi Beach Hotel, which provides most of the local nightlife; and the old village of cobbled streets, whitewashed cottages and bright flowers, is very attractive.

The mountains surrounding the village are good for walks, while the lively resort of Benítsai lies only five miles (8km) away and the bus runs to Corfu Town numerous times a day.

Accommodation

Hotel Albatros (tel: 55315). This relaxing 53-room 'B' grade hotel is opposite the sandy beach and about 10 minutes' walk from the centre of Moraitika. It has a medium-size pool with children's pool, a poolside bar and gardens. Only breakfast is served, but there is a choice of tavernas nearby.

Hotel Alkyonis (tel: 55201). A sister hotel of the Albatros, the 62-room 'B' grade Alkyonis is a five-minute walk from the beach. Guests can use the swimming pool at the Albatros. The hotel's colourful dining room offers an international and local menu, and the spacious public areas are cool and pleasantly decorated.

Hotel Capodistrias (tel: 55319). This is a delightful, 27-room grade 'B' hotel set in the hillside off the busy Benitsai road, opposite a narrow sand and shingle beach. The village centre is at least 20 minutes' walk away. The hotel is divided into six units, with four rooms to each unit, some with sea views, and the airy dining room offers three-course Greek menus that are highly rated by guests.

Hotel Delfinia (tel: 30318). An older-style 83-room 'A' grade hotel, it stands on its own stretch of shingle beach within a 10-minute walk of Moraïtika, and boasts a medium-size swimming pool set in gardens with plenty of shade. A log cabin-style restaurant in the grounds serves international and local dishes. Other facilities include a beach grill and bar, piano bar, electronic games, table tennis and television. The hotel also operates its own mini-bus service to Corfu Town twice daily.

Hotel Messonghi Beach (tel: 38684). Despite its name, this enormous (828 basically furnished rooms) 'B' class hotel/bungalow complex is in Moraïtika, not nearby Mesongi.

It is set in extensive grounds leading down to a sandy section of the beach. The centre of Moraïtika is within a 10-minute walk. The complex comprises several blocks, with accommodation in bungalows. The complex offers a wide range of amenities, including two medium-size swimming pools, a sun terrace, poolside bar, children's club and playground, and separate children's pool. A poolside self-service terrace grill offers hot dishes and salads. The entertainment programme ranges from bingo and television to discotheques, electronic games, tennis, a pool table, and keep fit. Watersports are available from the beach: in fact you need never leave the complex.

Hotel Miramare Beach (tel: 30183). This low-rise, 149-room deluxe hotel is situated on its own stretch of narrow beach just over 10 minutes' walk from Moraïtika, and has large gardens leading down to the beach, where there's a bar. Other amenities include a hairdressing salon, shop, television, billiards and a bar. The hotel operates a mini-bus service to Corfu Town.

Restaurants and Entertainment

The **Alkionis** is a smart, stylish restaurant in the centre of the resort, and enjoys an excellent reputation. Live music and plate smashing are features of the **Scorpion Disco**, while **Buddies** is noted for its wide variety of cocktails.

RESORTS

NISÁKI (NISSAKI)

Nisáki is a fishing hamlet nestling in the foothills of Mount Pandokrátor on Corfu's east coast, and is a favourite with travellers looking for a quiet holiday resort.

From the road, donkey tracks lead down steeply through the olive groves to the sea only a short distance away, and the resort offers a number of coves and sheltered bays with white pebble beaches, washed by waters of the most vivid blue and green. Boat hire, waterskiing, windsurfing, paragliding and most other watersports are available, and rustic waterfront tavernas serve satisfying, inexpensive meals.

Nisáki is one of the island's few resort areas which has managed to cling on to its original character, with peasants on donkeys still very much part of the scene. Apart from the Nissaki Beach Hotel and a few shops and tavernas spread along the busy, winding coastal road, there are limited facilities in the resort itself, so a hire car would be useful. The local bus to Corfu Town, about 14 miles (22km) south, travels through impressive scenery, and another popular excursion is to the pretty village of Kouloúra, a few miles north, with its wonderful views.

Accommodation

Club Med Helios (tel: 33381). A large, sprawling 'A' grade hotel complex, the Club Med stands on a hillside in a quiet, isolated position. Steep steps lead down to the hotel's private sandy beach which shelves quickly into deep water. The medium-size swimming pool (with children's section) is set in sun terraces, with a poolside bar and gardens. The hotel's large dining room enjoys a good reputation for its local and international dishes. As usual with Club Med developments, there is an extensive entertainment programme, ranging from nightly discotheques and live music to organised games and special evenings. Table tennis, tennis, aerobics, archery, green bowling, sailing, windsurfing, sub-aqua diving and waterskiing are all available, plus television, video films, electronic games and a pool table. There is also a souvenir shop and a hairdressing salon.

Hotel Nissaki Beach (tel: 91232). This 239-room 'A' grade hotel stands apart on its own shingle beach and is reached by a steep, winding road off the main coastal road. The large swimming pool and children's pool are set in a sun terrace, with poolside bar and gardens, including a children's playground. The large dining room serves international fare, and there's also a poolside Greek taverna. Other facilities include a discotheque, live music, a writing and card room, games room, tennis, table tennis, mini-golf, shops, a hairdressing salon and a beauty parlour. Good watersports facilities are available on the beach.

Restaurant

Vitamins on the outskirts of the resort has views over the bay, and serves reliable Greek and international food.

◆◆◆
PALAIOKASTRÍTSA
(PALEOKASTRITSA) ✓

Perhaps the most scenic spot in Corfu, Palaiokastrítsa (usually referred to simply as 'Paleo') is popular both as a resort in its own right and as an excursion destination, thanks not only to its setting but also to its numerous hotels, bars, tavernas and shops. It is spectacularly placed on the foothills of wooded mountains overlooking a beautiful bay. The resort fringes the northwestern coast of Corfu, about 15 miles (25km) from the capital, and has a friendly, easy-going atmosphere. It's a good choice for families and, because of its magnificent setting, is also popular with those who enjoy walking. Steep streets mean that it is not the place for anyone with walking difficulties.
'Paleo' owes much of its popularity to Sir Frederick Adam, British High Commissioner of the Ionian Islands, who in 1823 decided that the place would make an excellent picnic spot, and so ordered the building of a road for easy access. He justified the expense by putting forward a never-fulfilled plan to site a military convalescent home there! The road opened up the village, and it became popular with inveterate

travellers such as Elizabeth, Empress of Austria, Kaiser Wilhelm and Edward Lear. 'Paleo' offers four shingle bays, three of them with watersports facilities. The main bay tends to be the most crowded. One of the most popular excursions is a beach barbecue: a small fishing caique takes visitors to a remote cove for the day, with a lunch of charcoal-grilled chicken and lots of local wine. Another popular attraction is the *Kalypso Star*, a glass-bottomed boat which operates day and night cruises round

Palaiokastrítsa has a stunning setting – but be prepared for some steep walking

RESORTS

the bay in the peak season. The vessel is a trimaran specially designed for underwater viewing, and is fitted with powerful spotlights to let you see the underwater world after dark.

Perched on a rock overlooking the sea is the monastery of Theotokos, which lies at the end of the Adam road. It was founded in the 13th century, but the present buildings date from the 18th century. Inside the whitewashed walls, visitors may be offered a glass of refreshingly cold water by a monk at the old-fashioned well (open: 07.00 to 13.00 and 15.00 to 20.00; donations welcome). Beyond the lemon trees and carefully tended flower gardens is a pretty chapel. The one-room museum has some fantastic shells and huge bones extracted from the sea in the last century, as well as icons, several centuries old, and religious books. During the Middle Ages the monastery was linked to the fortress of Angelókastro, whose ruins are at the top of a steep hill behind. It was allegedly built by the Despot of Epiros, Angelos Komnenos, in the 13th century.

It is worth walking up to the fortress for its splendid views, but the less energetic will get good views from the Bella Vista Café, on a natural rock terrace about half way up. Offshore you will see a large rock, vaguely resembling a ship, which local tradition suggests is either Odysseus' ship, turned to stone by an angry Poseidon, or a

The rocky coast of 'Paleo' is best explored by boat

pirate ship turned to stone when it tried to rob the monastery. Good swimming can be enjoyed below the monastery and on Áyios Triadha beach, reached from the path near the Palaiokastritsa car hire office.

Excellent views can be enjoyed from a series of vantage points over several inlets and bays and towards the dramatic backdrop of mountains. A bus goes six times a day to Corfu Town and once on Sundays.

Accommodation
Hotel Akrotiri Beach (tel: 41275). This 126-room 'A'

international and local dishes, a regular discotheque, table tennis, television and electronic games. Windsurfing, pedaloes and boat rides are available on the beach.

Hotel Paleokastritsa (tel: 41207). This 163-room 'B' grade hotel is one of the best medium-size hotels in 'Paleo'. It stands above the resort but within a 10-minute walk of the nearest shingle beach, with fine views towards both the bay and the mountains. There's a medium-size swimming pool, a children's playground, and a large dining room furnished in local style and specialising in regional cuisine.

Liapades Beach Hotel (tel: 41294). This is a small three-storey pension-style hotel with a stretch of beach about 10 minutes' downhill walk away. There is a better beach about 20 minutes away, although this has no facilities, and 'Paleo' itself is about two miles (3km) away. Meals are taken at the taverna next door.

Oceanis Hotel (tel: 41229). A 71-room 'B' grade hotel built on a rocky outcrop overlooking one of Palaiokastritsa's bays, the Oceanis enjoys breathtaking views. The terrace and small swimming pool are popular with families, and the nearest beach is down a steep flight of steps. Interior decor and furnishings are best described as 'basic'. Watersports on nearby beaches include waterskiing, windsurfing, paragliding, pedaloes, canoes and snorkelling. The hotel has a bar, table tennis and electronic

grade hotel stands on a headland overlooking the sea, with a stretch of shingle beach, a five-minute downhill walk or a lift-ride away. The swimming pool is set in a cramped sun terrace, but there are two other sun terraces with good views. The small restaurant serves international fare and there's also a taverna which serves snacks. Entertainments include a discotheque, regular live music, video, table tennis and electronic games.

Hotel Elly Beach (tel: 41455). A modern, 48-room 'A' grade hotel complex set on its own shingle beach, the Elly Beach is about 30 minutes' walk from the resort. It has paved gardens and terraces, and offers games, and occasional evening entertainment.

Restaurants and Entertainment

By night holidaymakers and locals head for the many tavernas and bars, one of the most popular being the **Milde Sorte Club**, whose large terrace is covered by huge canopies. It is popular not only for its cuisine – especially fresh fish and seafood dishes – but also for its setting overlooking a bay.

Pirate's Bay is a good place to try a cocktail, while those who still have the energy but don't fancy the walk to **Paleo Disco**, on the outskirts of the resort, should look out for the orange caravanette which cruises along the main road offering 'lifts to the disco with the promise of a drive home afterwards.

◆◆
PÉRAMA

The small resort of Pérama lies north of Benítsai on both sides of the busy coastal road, with three good hotels and a number of bars and gift shops huddled together at the centre, and other hotels to the north and south.

It's a colourful resort, with bigger sisters Benítsai and Corfu Town conveniently close. One disadvantage is that there can be noise from the nearby airport, although this isn't nearly as much of a problem as it is at Kanóni, across the bay.

The centre of Pérama is small but offers many facilities: supermarkets, souvenir shops, tavernas, snack bars, pubs and cocktail bars. The atmosphere is friendly and relaxed. At night you can try some Greek dancing, and there are two local discotheques open until the early hours.

Beyond the centre, tavernas, bars and shops are scattered along the coastal road. There are small, shingly beaches to laze on, and watersports available include waterskiing, pedaloes and canoes. Paragliding can be tried in the southern part of the resort. Kanóni can be reached by a causeway, and makes a pleasant evening stroll, and Pérama is also well placed for trips to the Akhillion Palace (on the outskirts of Corfu Town) and to the small picturesque hill village of Gastoúrion, where Greek life goes on much as it has always done.

There is a good bus service to Corfu Town and Benítsai, with their wide range of facilities and night-time distractions, and to the southern resorts of Mesongí and Kavos.

Accommodation

Hotel Aeolos Beach (tel: 33132). This 346-room 'B' grade hotel, within 10 minutes' walk of its own beach, stands above the main coastal road, with Pérama a 15-minute walk away. The medium-size swimming pool is set in a small sun terrace area, with a poolside bar. Facilities include a children's playground, beachside snackbar, discotheque, electronic games, mini-golf, card room and television. Watersports

The gardens of the Aeolos Beach Hotel, Pérama

are available from the beach, and the dining room offers special menus for children.
Hotel Alexandros (tel: 36855). Right in the heart of Pérama, within a 10-minute walk of its own shingle beach, the 88-room 'A' grade hotel offers a medium-size swimming pool set in secluded gardens, a poolside bar/taverna, a discotheque, card room, television, electronic games, table tennis,

and regular barbecues. There is also a shop and hairdressing salon.
Hotel Oasis (tel: 38190). This 'B' grade 67-room family-run hotel is also in the centre of Pérama, and looks down to its own shingle beach. Among the hotel's features are gardens, a discotheque, and electronic games.
Hotel Pontikonnisi (tel: 36871). Directly below the flight path for the airport, the Pontikonnisi is an attractive small 'C' grade hotel on the coast road, but suffers from aircraft noise. Six

RESORTS

storeys high, with levels terraced down to its own small pebble and rock beach, it has a dining room with views across the bay, as well as a discotheque. A bus stop for Corfu Town is near by, and the centre of Pérama is a 10-minute walk away.

Restaurants and Entertainment

'Cheers' is recommended for an inexpensive snack, and Zeffiros is good for Greek food. Inland of Pérama, in the village of Kinopiástai, is one of Corfu's most respected restaurants, the Tripa. It offers a set menu of an unusually high standard, together with a variety of live entertainment each night, and is popular with both Corfiots and visitors from all parts of the island.

◆

PLÁTONAS (PLATANOS)

A small, inland residential area with one hotel, Plátonas is about one and a half miles (2½ km) south of the resort of Ródha, in the northern part of Corfu. Buses run several times a day to Ródha, which has a sand and shingle beach, and to Corfu Town, 22 miles (35km) away. Bicycles can be hired at the resort and there is pony trekking just outside it.

Accommodation

Hotel Platanos (tel: 94396). The Platanos is a small, quiet 'D' grade hotel popular with young singles and those seeking good value. The medium-size swimming pool has a terrace and poolside bar, and there are pleasant gardens. Meals are

limited to breakfast, but poolside snacks and barbecues are available. There is a good bar, a weekly discotheque, table tennis, electronic games, television and video films.

RÓDHA (RODA)

Ródha is a small resort in northern Corfu, and appeals to families looking for a beach holiday. The recent building of apartments and village rooms throughout the centre means that it is becoming an increasingly lively resort, however.

It has a narrow sandy beach and a handful of gift shops and tavernas, as well as two discotheques. The town lies to the right of the coast road some 22 miles (35km) north of Corfu Town, to which buses run four times a day and once on Sundays.

Accommodation

Hotel Milton (tel: 49081). This is a 24-room 'C' grade hotel in a quiet position, 15 minutes from the sand and shingle beach and the resort centre. Facilities include a medium-size swimming pool with a sun terrace, and electronic games. Hotel Roda Beach (tel: 93202). This 388-room 'B' grade hotel is at the end of a poor, dusty road some 20 minutes from Ródha, which can also be approached along the sand and shingle beach. There are two main blocks of three and four floors, with extra bungalow accommodation in the grounds. Extensive gardens lead down to the beach. Features include two swimming pools (one suitable for children), a sun terrace, a card room, table tennis, electronic games, pool table, and mini-golf.

Hotel Silver Beach (tel: 63112). A 33-room, family-owned 'C' grade hotel within five minutes' walk of a stretch of sandy beach, the Silver Beach offers high standards and good value. It has a medium-size swimming pool, sun terraces, a poolside bar and gardens.

◆◆
SIDHÁRI (SIDARI)

Not so many years ago Sidhári, situated on Corfu's northwestern coast some 24 miles (39km) from the island's capital, was a small fishing hamlet noted only for its long sandy beaches. Today, it has blossomed into a friendly little holiday resort offering

Erosion has created coves and rock formations at Sidhári

something for just about everyone.

From Corfu Town the resort is reached by a road which climbs the Troumbetta Pass and then descends through traditional villages, before running through a lush valley to the centre of Sidhári, on its sweeping bay.

Sidhári has beaches of soft golden sand, and the sea is said to be the warmest to be found around the island. The water is shallow and safe for non-swimmers. Watersports are becoming increasingly popular here, and it is possible to rent pedaloes, canoes and sailing dinghies. Waterskiing and paragliding are also available, and there are trips along the coast by a glass-bottomed boat.

In the bay is the 'Canal d'Amour', a channelled rock formation, said to be two lovers turned to stone. Any couple swimming through it is

RESORTS

Inland scenery near Sidhári is as beautiful as the coast

promised eternal love! It is one of a number of strange rock formations caused by the erosion of the sandstone cliffs, and there are also secluded sandy coves nestling between the steep, craggy rocks, reached by footpaths which run over the gorse-covered hillocks.

In the evenings you can relax over a meal at one of the many open-air tavernas and seafood restaurants, and then move on for cakes, coffee and brandy at the patisserie or visit one of the surprisingly good music bars or two discotheques.

Excursions are available by boat around the coast to either Kassiópi or Palaiokastrítsa, and you can also visit the almost deserted westernmost Greek islands of Erikoúsa, Othonoí and Mathráki (enquire at Sidhári's tour offices for schedules). Inland is a network of rivers, lush pastures, woodlands and lovely villages such as Magouládhes and Kounavádhes.

Buses run to Corfu Town five times a day but not on Sundays.

Accommodation
Hotel Selas (tel: 95285) This quiet 'C' grade 21-room hotel is within a 10-minute walk of

shingle beach, with its front entrance facing the narrow main street. It has a sun terrace, discotheque and live music, and serves local cuisine.

Restaurants and Entertainment

The **Oasis** and the **Sophocles** are both popular restaurants, while the best and liveliest discotheques are probably **Legends**, **Three Brothers** and the **Canal d'Amour**. The **Crocodile** bar serves food and drink to the accompaniment of videos, while the **Pipistrelo Pub** has music every night and regular Greek evenings.

◆

YIALISKÁRI (YALISCARI)

Yialiskári is a peaceful resort, with impressive scenery, a few miles south of its bigger and better-known neighbour Glifádha. Another isolated west coast resort, it is dominated by one hotel – the Yaliscari Palace – and is approximately seven miles (11km) from Corfu Town. Within 15 minutes' drive from the resort is the unspoilt town of Sinarádhes, with a History and Folklore Museum of Central Corfu (open during the summer season, but closed Mondays). Áyioi Dhéka, Corfu's second highest mountain, is a drive and a walk away, and affords excellent views of the island and coast.

Accommodation

Hotel Yaliscari Palace (tel: 54401). This stylish 'A' grade hotel has 226 rooms, and lies at the end of a winding tree-lined approach road. The shingle beach is a 20-minute walk

the centre of Sidhári, up a narrow, unmade road, and is within five minutes of the wide, sandy beach. It has a medium-size pool with poolside bar.
Hotel Sidari Beach (tel: 95216). The Sidari is an 80-room 'C' grade family-owned hotel on a stretch of sand and shingle beach, with views of the sea and mountains. Sidhári itself is a 20-minute walk away. Among the hotel's amenities are a small sun terrace off the bar area, electronic games and television and board games. International food is served.
Hotel Three Brothers (tel: 95342). Originally a taverna, this 36-room family-run 'C' grade hotel backs onto a small

RESORTS

down a steep track, and the hotel also runs a mini-bus shuttle service to the beach. Facilities include a medium-size outdoor swimming pool and a small indoor pool. Babysitting can be arranged, as can early meals for children. Discotheques, live music and occasional folk music evenings are held; and the hotel has shops and a hairdressing salon. Watersports are available from the beach, and the Corfu Golf Club is within easy reach.

PAXOÍ (PAXOS)

One of the most popular excursions for holidaymakers in Corfu is a boat trip to the island of Paxoí, about 30 miles (48km) away. It is also an increasingly popular holiday destination in its own right. According to mythology, Poseidon, god of the seas, created Paxoí as an idyllic retreat for himself and his beloved Amphitriti by striking off the southern part of Corfu with a mighty blow of his trident. Another version is that, seeking a resting place on his voyage from Corfu to Lefkas, Poseidon struck his trident and Paxoí emerged through the Ionian waters. It immediately attracted a host of seabirds and other marine creatures.

Paxoí: sleepy villages, sunbleached rocks and about a quarter of a million olive trees

Just seven miles long and about two wide (11km by 5km) with Megali Vigla at St Isavros the highest point at 820ft (250m) above sea level, Paxoí is the smallest real island of the Ionian group. Its sister island of Andípaxoí (Antipaxos) is only a quarter its size, and there are a number of outlying islets tinier still. After the opulence of parts of Corfu, Paxoí feels refreshingly unsophisticated. In Gáios, for instance, the bank doubles as an ironmonger's store!

The island's landscape is wild and rugged, gentle and rolling and is carpeted with olive, pine and cypress trees right up to its shores. Countless tracks through the olive groves peter out in lazy whitewashed hamlets or at quiet, tree-backed beaches. These many tracks provide plenty of scope for artists and make beautiful walks, especially in the spring and autumn when there is a mass of wild flowers and the heady fragrance of blossom is in the air. There is no end of small churches to hunt out, as well as some disused olive presses and windmills. Andípaxoí, too, has its share of churches and also vineyards, tended by the Paxiots for local wine production. You can hire a small boat with an outboard engine to explore the coast, and caiques depart regularly for trips around Paxoí and to Andípaxoí, Mourtos, Pargo and Corfu.

The Paxoí coastline is spectacular, and there are numerous unspoilt beaches, mainly pebble bays and rocky coves, some inaccessible by land, with plenty of scope for swimming, snorkelling and fishing. There are also fascinating sea caves and impressive natural rock formations at Brimitus on the west coast. Also on the west coast are the Seven Seas Caves, the best known of which is Ipperandi. Homer said this was the sea god Poseidon's cave.

There are three main coastal villages, all linked by buses: Lákka in the north, Longós in the north east, and Gáios, the capital, in the south east. Tourists are welcomed everywhere and made to feel at home. Nobody is too busy to spare the time to answer a question, and after a hard day's swimming and sunbathing you can linger in the tavernas over an informal meal of Paxiot specialities: fresh lobster, perhaps, or delicious pastries.

RESORTS

Gáios

The approach to Gáios is unforgettable, as the ferry slowly makes its way along the natural aquamarine channel between Paxoí and the miniscule islet of Áyios Nikólaos. Gáios is the capital of Paxoí and a natural venue for yachts and other small vessels. It has a cheerful waterfront square, lined with small boutiques and stores.

Gáios is under a preservation order which helps to retain its old world character. For the most part it is a quiet, sleepy place, except in the high season when daytrippers from Corfu crowd the pretty harbour for a few hours. It attracts a mixture of nationalities, with life centring around the few bars and tavernas of the main square. During the summer they serve fresh fish and sometimes lobster. The main building in the village is the small white-washed church, outside which the village priest is often to be found, sitting in a wicker chair.

Longós

Longós, a 15-minute bus or taxi drive north from Gáios, is a small, peaceful fishing village with some good fish tavernas. It is just a few minutes' walk to the nearest shingle beach.

Lákka

Lákka, which lies further north, is a lively little village with several tavernas and bars, and the Aloni Disco. Days in Lákka are inevitably spent on the beach – a shingle bay where watersports are available, reached through an olive grove. Take time to visit the village's pride and joy – a small aquarium where a couple of knowledgeable guides take work to heart.

Accommodation

Paxos Beach Hotel (tel: 0662) 32211). This 42-room 'B' grade hotel is built against the hillside on the outskirts of Gáios, surrounded by olive trees, and enjoys panoramic views over the sea. The setting is tranquil, with Gáios about 15 minutes' walk away. Accommodation is in small blocks of bungalows. A flight of steps leads to the pebbly beach, while Mongoníssi, another bay, is a five-minute drive away.

Restaurants and Entertainment

The high standard of food on Paxoí is exemplified at the **Amnesia** on the square in Gáios, and **Taka Taki** close by. In Lákka, the **Petalouda**, **Pantheon** and **Klinis** are recommended. For entertainment, there are a couple of discos, of which **Phoenix** is 'the' place to be seen. From the good selection of tavernas, **Dodo's** is probably the most reliable.

How to Get to Paxoí

Numerous tour operators are now offering stay-put holidays in Paxoí, while scores of travel agencies throughout Corfu organise excursions to the island of varying duration. In either case, Paxoí is reached by ferry from Corfu Town to Gáios, a journey of about three hours. A local bus connects Gáios with Longós and Lákka.

PEACE AND QUIET

Corfu's Countryside and Wildlife
by Paul Sterry

For those who enjoy peace and quiet and who have an interest in natural history, Corfu is an ideal holiday destination. Although holiday centres and resort beaches may be crowded, drive a few miles along the coast or inland and you will still find sleepy villages, deserted coves and beautiful hillsides dotted with olive groves and stately funeral cypress trees. Here you can study a wealth of flowers, insects and birds, or simply relax in solitude and enjoy this most idyllic of Ionian Islands. One of the first visitors to be captivated by Corfu and its natural history was Gerald Durrell. His accounts of a childhood spent studying natural history have entertained many people, and few of those who have read his books, and later visited the island, find it any less enthralling.

Corfu's coastline is understandably the highlight of a visit for many people. The largely unspoilt west coast has beaches, rocky headlands and dramatic cliffs, all bathed in the azure waters of the Mediterranean. Do venture inland, however, because freshwater marshes, colourful *maquis* vegetation and meadows, and a limestone mountain all hold their own plants and animals to delight the naturalist.

The British cemetery in Corfu Town is a green paradise, with many orchids among its flowers

PEACE AND QUIET

The Coast and Sea

Corfu's coastline is as delightful as it is varied. Although a few areas have been developed to such an extent that they have lost their appeal, many of the island's beaches, coves and cliffs are, to all intents and purposes, unspoilt. The shape of Corfu also ensures that, wherever you are, you are never very far from the sea, and, indeed, the deep blue waters of the Mediterranean can be seen from most of the best wildlife areas.

At one time, the coastline would have harboured both loggerhead turtles and monk seals. Disturbance of former turtle nesting areas and the

The blue rock thrush has a pretty song and lives mainly on insects – and the occasional lizard

hunting of seals by fishermen mean that a sighting of either species is now a rare event. However, a wealth of colourful and extraordinary marine creatures still survives in the seas around Corfu, most of them only a few inches below the surface of the water.

The Mediterranean has little tidal range, so there are few opportunities to explore rock pools. However, with the aid of a simple snorkel or a net you can soon find starfishes, blennies, sea urchins, sea slugs and many more. Always remember to return anything you catch to the sea; marine animals soon die if kept out of the water.

Because of the unspoilt nature of much of the coast, *maquis* vegetation often descends almost to sea level. Much of this flourishing coastal landscape is dotted with the characteristic tall, thin shapes of funeral cypress trees, and with maritime pines, both of which are favoured by serins as song perches. Close to the sea, maritime plants such as rock samphire, buckshorn plantain, sea lavender and the introduced hottentot fig thrive in rocky areas, while, along the landward side of sandy beaches, sea medick, sea beet, spurges and sea stocks predominate.

In common with most of the Mediterranean region, the variety of birdlife around the coast is rather limited. Periods of severe onshore winds may bring passing gulls, cormorants, Cory's shearwaters and Yelkouan shearwaters close to land, but seldom in any numbers. Where vegetation clings to the cliffs, a few warblers may be found and blue rock thrushes sing from rocky outcrops. Lucky visitors may witness the flying skills of a peregrine or an Eleonora's falcon hunting for small birds close to the cliff face.

Olive Groves and Agricultural Land

One of the most enduring memories of a holiday on Corfu is the rolling landscape dotted with gnarled and twisted olive trees: there are said to be more than three million on the island! Their grey-green leaves shimmer in the heat of the day, the shady groves providing welcome relief from the Mediterranean sun and supporting an underlying carpet of colourful and abundant wild flowers. Many of Corfu's birds find sanctuary in these groves, the foliage not only providing shade from the sun but also supporting large numbers of insects which serve as food. Cicadas are without doubt the most audible insects among the olive groves, although they are the most difficult to see. These skilled ventriloquists sing incessantly throughout spring and summer, and yet attempts to pinpoint the sources of the sounds are seldom successful. Their larval stages are subterranean, and an early morning search of trunks and stems may yield fresh adults newly emerged beside the dried remains of their nymphal

A woodchat shrike prepares to rub a bee on barbed wire, to remove its sting

skins. This temporary immobility does not last long, however, and they soon take to the wing. After dark, a different songster can be heard among the olive groves. All night, Scop's owls utter their monotonous whistling call which bears an uncanny resemblance to the 'blips' of sonar.

In spring, songbirds abound among the olive groves. Migrant species, some of which stay to breed and some of which continue their journey north after a short stay, are most noticeable in April and May. Blackcaps, nightingales, olive-tree warblers, olivaceous warblers, spotted flycatchers, collared flycatchers, black-headed buntings and woodchat shrikes are among the most regularly encountered birds as they forage for insects or establish territories with loud songs. Shady streams and pools beneath the trees often lure thirsty birds to drink and bathe, while butterflies are attracted to the concentration of salt at the drying margins. Fortunately for visitors to Corfu, its agriculture is far from intensive, and this is reflected in the wealth of wild flowers to be found growing alongside crop plants. In our own gardens we would call them weeds, but here they are an essential part of the landscape. Meadows beneath olive groves are often left to be grazed by sheep or goats, and in spring are full of corn marigolds, field marigolds, crown daisies, southern daisies, herb robert, lesser bugloss, red and white clovers, gladioli, orchids and anemones.

Open Country

Visitors to Corfu might be forgiven for assuming that the vegetation of this delightful island is the same as it ever was. Although comparatively little real change has taken place in the landscape over the last thousand years or so, prior to man's colonisation of Corfu it would have been cloaked largely in evergreen forests. Cleared for firewood, agriculture and villages, these forests are now reduced to pockets of evergreen oaks and pines, but the vegetation that has replaced them is still of great interest to the visiting naturalist.

Olive groves and tilled fields retain the hallmark of man's influence. However, most areas which have been ignored or abandoned to grazing sheep and goats following woodland felling, have developed a rich, shrubby habitat known to botanists as *maquis*. Characterised by plants such as kermes oak, strawberry tree, lentisc, tree heathers, sage leaved cistus, myrtle, juniper, butcher's broom, asparagus, rosemary and brooms, the habitat is recognisable by its smell alone. A heady mixture of fragrances greets the nose and is reminiscent as much of the kitchen as of the perfumery. Desiccation is a real problem for Corfu's plants, compounded by nibbling by animals. Aromatic oils in the leaves help reduce water evaporation but may, in some species, also put off herbivores. Fearsome spines on plants such as *Smilax aspera* and bramble also serve as deterrents, as anyone who has walked through the *maquis* will testify.

The *maquis* fragrances appeal to most insects, and this habitat can be especially good for butterflies. Camberwell beauties, eastern orange tips, green hairstreaks, southern white admirals, long-tailed blues, dappled whites and cleopatras are among the many colourful species that may be encountered. Reptiles also abound in the *maquis*: Hermann's tortoises, Balkan wall lizards, Montpellier snakes, four-lined snakes and leopard snakes all occur, but are often too active and wary to be seen well.

The birdlife of the open country is equally varied, although

The dappled white is one of the many butterflies attracted to Corfu's rich plant life

some species are difficult to see. Bee-eaters, magpies and hooded crows are generally conspicuous, but not so the habitat's smaller inhabitants, such as Sardinian warblers, subalpine warblers and spectacled warblers. Quiet, patient observation, preferably early in the morning, is often the only way to get good views of these skulking species. Kestrels are the most prominent birds of prey on the island, but, during migration times, study each one carefully: red-footed falcons and lesser kestrels pass through.

Mount Pandokrátor
At 2,970 feet (906m) above sea level, Mount Pandokrátor

(Pantokrator) is the highest point on the island of Corfu. By many country's standards this may not be especially high, but the altitude is enough to moderate the summer temperatures and to encourage a rich growth of plants. Although a dusty road now leads to the summit, the best opportunities for the naturalist are had by parking just beyond the village of Perithia and completing the journey on foot: many of the more interesting plants will be found in this way. When the summit of Pandokrátor is finally reached, panoramic views encompass the village below and surrounding farmland, and stretch all the way to the coast of Albania and beyond. Mount Pandokrátor is on the itinerary of most botanists who visit Corfu. Part of the reason for its attraction lies in the altitude, but the underlying rock, namely limestone, is also a significant factor. The well-drained, alkaline soils are thin and do not suit all types of plant. However, many thrive in these conditions, and orchids, such as man orchids, monkey orchids, four-spotted orchids, yellow bee orchids, brown bee orchids and toothed orchids, are abundant in April and May. The summit also boasts a wide range of other flowers, such as gladioli, irises, grape hyacinths, crocuses and thistles, as well as abundant anemones, Greek fritillaries, which grow in the ancient terraces, and an endemic, autumn-flowering species of snowdrop.

For the birdwatcher, Mount Pandokrátor is comparatively dull. Small parties of swifts are sometimes joined by Alpine swifts, while larger species are generally represented by ravens or hooded crows. Buzzards occasionally soar overhead on outstretched wings, and may be joined in spring and autumn by migrant birds of prey, such as honey buzzard, hobby, osprey or short-toed eagle. However, these pass through quickly and often at great height, so identification may be difficult. As you descend from the summit, tracks pass through dense scrub and agricultural land. Asphodels, marigolds, thistles and poppies mark your progress and, in spring, Sardinian warblers, whitethroats, blackcaps and nightingales sing or scold from

Mount Pandokrátor is rich in limestone-loving plants, including several types of orchid

almost every clump of trees or bushes that you pass.

Límni Koríssia

Límni Koríssia (Lake Korission) is a large, shallow lake which lies in the southwest of Corfu and is well worth visiting, both for its natural history interest and as a good place to relax. Not only do the margins of the lake and its waters teem with life, but the sand dunes which separate Koríssia from the sea have been colonised by a wealth of interesting plants and

insects. Fortunately, access is easy and cars can be driven to the edge of the lake. Thereafter, all you need is keen eyesight and perhaps a pair of binoculars.

With freshwater at such a premium on Corfu, it is not surprising that Limni Korissia attracts large numbers of waterbirds. Waders such as wood sandpipers, dunlin, common sandpipers, ruff, greenshank, black-winged stilts and avocets are sometimes joined by species more usually associated with the seashore, like turnstones and grey plovers. Little egrets are often seen, and lucky observers may find the occasional great egret or glossy ibis, especially if they have the additional aid of a telescope.

Collared pratincoles and small flocks of white-winged black terns sometimes pass through on migration, as do groups of garganey. This elegant duck migrates south to Africa for the winter, when it is replaced on Limni Korissia by other wildfowl such as teal, shelduck, mallard, shoveler and wigeon. Winter is also the most interesting season for unusual gulls, such as Audouin's or Mediterranean gulls.

The marshy margins to the lake and sand dunes are home to flowers such as the Mediterranean catchfly, *Silene colorata*, and Jersey orchids in spring, while spikes of sea daffodil appear in the autumn. Closer to the sea, the flora becomes more maritime and includes species such as purple spurge, which sprawls across the sand and gravel, sea spurge, sea stock, sea holly and clumps of cottonweed, an aptly named plant cloaked in downy hairs. Lizards and grasshoppers abound here, and the mole cricket sometimes emerges briefly from its subterranean tunnels before retreating underground again. Tawny pipits and short-toed larks hunt for insects among the sandy hollows and Kentish plovers lay their eggs in shallow nest scrapes, often in surprisingly public places.

Alikes Saltpans

The saltpans at Alikes, on the shores of the Bay of Levkimmi in the south of Corfu, are a wonderful excursion for visitors with an interest in birdwatching: the network of pools and drying pans attracts thousands of waders, herons, egrets and wildfowl. Although the spring and autumn migration periods are best in terms of variety, the winter months also have their highlights, and it is only during the height of summer that the number of birds is small. Spring migration lasts from March until May. Some birds stay only a few hours to rest

and feed, while others may linger for several days or weeks. One of the first to arrive, and also one of the easiest to recognise, is the black winged stilt. Its long, red legs enable it to wade into deep water to catch aquatic animals with its needle-like bill. Black and white avocets are also straightforward to identify, but not so some of the other waders. Ruff, redshanks, greenshanks, wood sandpipers, marsh sandpipers, little stints, grey plovers, little ringed plovers and Kentish plovers can look confusingly similar at a distance and to the untrained eye. However, visitors in spring should take heart from the knowledge that identification of these species in autumn plumage is even more difficult!

Mediterranean gulls are occasional winter visitors and sometimes stay on into the spring. Their white wings and characteristic 'cow-cow' call makes them easy to tell from superficially similar black-headed gulls. Several species of terns may also pass through on migration, their buoyant flight distinguishing them from gulls.

Little egrets can also be seen at Alikes. Their all-white plumage makes them easy to spot at a distance, while their black legs and bright yellow feet separate them from larger great egrets. As with anywhere on a migration route, unusual species sometimes turn up. Flamingoes, glossy ibises and white storks may stay briefly in spring or autumn. Yellow wagtails are often abundant, with several European races, such as blue-headed and black-headed wagtails, often being found. Any small bird that looks slightly different should be studied closely: it might turn out to be a red-throated pipit.

Áyios Spirídhon

Áyios Spirídhon, in northern Corfu, is considered by many wildlife enthusiasts to be one of the most interesting areas on the island. Although birdwatching is undoubtedly the highlight, with reed-fringed wetlands and adjacent scrub acting as havens for migrants and breeding species alike, flowers can be found in profusion together with

The bright yellow spots of the European pond terrapin provide surprisingly effective camouflage

butterflies, reptiles and amphibians. The setting is wonderful: the inviting, azure waters of the Mediterranean provide a beautiful contrast to the backdrop of the green slopes of Mount Pandokrátor, which lies inland.

In spring, marsh harriers gracefully quarter the reedbeds in search of prey, perhaps staying in the area to breed on occasions. Purple herons, grey herons, night herons, squacco herons and little bitterns are generally less easy to see, as they often remain hidden in the vegetation. They catch their prey by creeping quietly through the reeds, but sometimes they venture into the open or fly from one area of marsh to another, and provide good views for the patient observer. European pond terrapins bask beside

PEACE AND QUIET

the water and are sometimes difficult to spot because of their immobility. However, this inertia quickly disappears at the slightest sign of danger, when they dive beneath the water's surface with a loud 'splosh'.

At Áyios Spiridhon, Corfu's usual background serenade of cicadas is sometimes drowned by the chorus of marsh frogs and tree frogs. These all have to compete with the songs of migrant reed warblers, great reed warblers and sedge warblers and the incessant 'zip-zip-zip' of resident fantailed warblers. This latter species is easily recognised, despite its small size, both by its song and its mode of delivery: the bird flies high above its territory and sings as if suspended from a yo-yo.

Aromatic scrubland vegetation at Áyios Spiridhon appeals to swallowtail butterflies

The colourful *maquis* scrub which borders the Áyios Spiridhon's marshes is an excellent area for newly arrived migrant birds. The proximity of the island to the mainland means that many more species pass through than stay to breed. Chats and warblers, such as subalpine, olivaceous and olive-tree warblers, rest and feed in comparatively low-growing scrub, while larger bushes and olive groves harbour flycatchers, woodchat shrikes, great grey shrikes, nightingales and golden orioles. As elsewhere on the island, early mornings provide the best opportunities for the birdwatcher.

The *maquis* vegetation comprises a range of characteristic plants such as cistuses, brooms, rosemary and heathers, but the Áyios Spiridhon area is particularly good for orchids. Several species of tongue orchids occur, often appearing as complex hybrids, which hinders their identification. Colourful spikes of Jersey orchids prefer damp ground, but the several members of the bee orchid family which occur are generally found in drier and more open terrain.

The colourful and often aromatic vegetation is a riot of colour from February to May, and attracts a wide range of insects, from day-flying hummingbird hawk moths and rose chafer beetles to butterflies such as green hairstreaks, small coppers, clouded yellows and southern

A roller can sometimes be seen travelling through in spring and autumn

swallowtails. Grasshoppers and bush crickets scurry among the foliage, and sometimes fall victim to the vice-like grip and ferocious mandibles of praying mantids.

Bird Migration
Spring sees the arrival in northern Europe of hundreds of thousands of migrant birds which have spent the winter months in Africa. The Mediterranean is a major obstacle in their path, and Corfu's position on the northern coast ensures that many of these tired migrants stop off, albeit briefly, to feed and rest. Some intrepid species fly directly across the open sea and make Corfu their first landfall. Others fly up the coast of Greece, and the island's close proximity to the mainland attracts a wider range of migrant species than are found on most other Greek islands.

Spring migration is at a peak from late March until early May, although stragglers may occur as late as June. The return migration, however, is more protracted, and often lasts from August well into October. If the weather is fine, many birds will pass straight over the island, but a short spell of bad weather often grounds hundreds of individuals. Songbirds tend to head for the first cover they come across, so areas of scrub or orchards around the coast are especially productive. Áyios Spirídhon and Sidhári, in the north of the island, and from Límni Koríssia to Levkímmi in the south are worth searching for migrants, particularly in the first few hours of daylight, during the migration months.

PEACE AND QUIET

Compared with most Greek islands, Corfu has a good range of nesting songbirds, many of which arrive in spring for the summer months. However, the list of breeding birds is swollen dramatically by passage migrants, which pass through on a regular basis. Blackcaps, whitethroats, subalpine warblers, Orphean warblers, olivaceous warblers and olive-tree warblers can usually be found by careful searching, along with black-headed buntings, whinchats, spotted flycatchers, red-breasted flycatchers, collared flycatchers and pied flycatchers.

Swallows, red-rumped swallows and sand martins arrive in March and April, but perhaps the most characteristic birds of spring are the bee-eaters. Small parties of these incredibly colourful birds arrive in early May and hunt insects on the wing while uttering their liquid calls. Equally colourful, but less frequent, are rollers, which pass through in spring and again in autumn. These dumpy, blue birds are sometimes seen perched on overhead wires or on dead branches.

Corfu's Wild Flowers

Corfu has a well-deserved reputation as the greenest of the Greek Islands. Compared to the Aegean Islands, Mediterranean islands in general and, indeed, other Ionian Islands, such as Zakinthos and Cephalonia, Corfu's vegetation is lush.

Although parts of the island do become dry and parched during the summer months, these soon burst into life with the autumn rains. Whereas most Mediterranean islands do not become green again until December, Corfu has a colourful array of flowers by October.

The climate of the Mediterranean, with its dry, hot summers and mild, wet winters, has had a profound effect on the native plants. Most are either drought-resistant or wither away above ground during the hottest months. Winter is generally the growing season, but on Corfu, with its higher than average rainfall and protracted season, growth starts much earlier. The climate is influenced by the island's close proximity to the mountains of Greece and Albania, and many more species flower in autumn than elsewhere in the Mediterranean. This, in effect, creates a second 'spring', and many keen botanists make one trip in spring and one in autumn to do it justice.

The spring flowering period on Corfu lasts from February until May with a succession of colourful and fascinating species putting in appearances. By searching the island's hilly and mountainous regions, the botanist can often find early flowering species, long-since 'over' around the coast, in bloom at higher altitudes. Gladioli, grape hyacinths, anemones, marigolds, asphodels, squills, bellflowers, poppies and

*Always green, Corfu becomes a
mass of colour in April and May*

cranesbills are all abundant
but often require considerable
effort and a good field guide to
determine their specific
identity. For the orchid
enthusiast, April and May are
by far the best months for
variety.

Autumn brings new rewards
for the botanist. Around the
coast, sea squills and sea
daffodils produce spikes of
flowers from the most barren
and unpromising soils.

Elsewhere, rocky soils, grassy
fields and shady paths are all
productive. Beautiful patches of
yellow sternbergia can be
found, along with bellflowers,
crocuses, narcissi, meadow
saffron and the delicate spikes
of autumn lady's tresses, a late-
flowering orchid.

Wild Orchids
Wild orchids hold a great
fascination for many people.
Part of the intrigue lies in their
strangely beautiful flowers and
peculiar life-histories, and part
in their rarity value. While

PEACE AND QUIET

*Reinhold's orchid is one of
several that look like bees*

Corfu may be a wonderful
place for the orchid enthusiast,
the latter criterion can hardly
be said to apply, because over
30 species and numerous
subspecies occur on the island.
In the right places and at the
right time of year, many
species are nothing short of
abundant.
Like all wildflowers on Corfu,
orchids should be admired and
perhaps photographed but
never picked. They, more than
most plants, deserve a special
reverence, because most
species take several years to
grow from seed to the
flowering stage. It takes only a
few seconds to destroy them
with a thoughtless act.
Among the most numerous and
most attractive of Corfu's
orchids are members of the
bee orchid family, *Ophrys*.

Horseshoe, Reinhold's, early
spider, woodcock, sawfly and
yellow bee orchids are all
widespread on open, sunny
slopes, and most can be found
in flower between March and
May. Although each species
has characteristic features, the
identification of some hybrid
specimens may prove
impossible. The flowers of
many *Ophrys* species bear
striking resemblances to
wasps and bumblebees,
insects which often serve as
pollinating agents for these
extraordinary plants.
Many of the larger species of
orchids belong to the family
Orchis, and Jersey, toothed,
lady and pink butterfly orchids,
as well as those with more
unusual names, such as naked
man orchid and monkey
orchid, all occur. Several
species of *Serapias* or tongue
orchids and the extraordinary
lizard orchid can also be found
in April and May, flowering
long after spikes of the aptly
named giant orchid have
withered away.
If time is limited, the orchid
enthusiast should not miss the
grounds of the British
Cemetery in Corfu Town.
Here, among the graves and
urns full of gladioli, over 25
species of orchid have, at one
time or another, been
recorded, some no doubt
'encouraged' to take root by
careful introduction. If you tire
of the wildflowers, the
cemetery is sometimes good
for migrant birds in spring or
autumn, and is always a quiet
and peaceful spot to spend a
few hours.

FOOD AND DRINK

Because of the popularity of
Corfu among British
holidaymakers, many holiday
hotels and restaurants serve
'international' fare to please
British tastes, such as chicken,
lamb chops, sausage-egg-and-
chips and the like, and there
are often special children's
meals. However, many
establishments also offer
Greek cuisine as an alternative,
and this is often of a high
standard.

Greek restaurants (*estiatória*)
and tavernas are virtually
indistinguishable on Corfu.
Tavernas abound throughout
Corfu, most of them
representing excellent value. A
smart appearance is by no
means a good indication of
quality – in fact, the more basic
tavernas are often the best,
especially if they are
frequented by the locals. Even
if you cannot understand the
menu, you may be invited into
the kitchen to make a choice
from the dishes you see being
prepared.

A *psistaria* specialises in meats
grilled over charcoal, and, in
resorts, may double as a fast
food joint serving pizzas,
toasted sandwiches and
hamburgers. In town you may
find small shops selling Greek
fast food.

If your taste is more
wholesome, the *galaktopolian*
(dairy) is the place, serving
milk, yoghurt, custards and
milk puddings, but it is not
open during the evening. Fish
(*psari*) such as lobster,
crayfish, shrimps, squid and
swordfish, seems keenly
priced to many visitors,
although it is no longer the
staple food of the locals:
pollution and overfishing of the
seas have made prices rise.
Although menus are often
limited in choice, there is
usually lamb, pork and chicken
on offer. Those unaccustomed
to Greek food may find it a little
oily, but the olive oil is used not
soley for cooking but as a
flavouring. The Corfiots seem
to prefer their meals served
warm rather than hot which is
suited to the hot climate. The
olive oil pressed in Corfu is
among the best in the
Mediterranean – a wonderful
green colour and smooth in
texture and taste. The oranges
of the island are also very good
and the wild strawberries are a
delight.

Tsintsinbeera is a word that may
puzzle, but is another British
legacy – ginger beer, and
more like true ginger beer than
anything to be found on sale in
present day Britain. *Kek* (cake)
usually means a heavy and
delicious type of plum and fruit
cake.

Greek Cuisine

Menus are often in Greek,
English, French and German
and will offer a limited choice
that includes *mezedes* (hors
d'oeuvres) and *tis oras* (meat
and fish fried or grilled to
order).

Since the idea of courses is
foreign to Greek cuisine,
starters, main dishes and salads
often arrive together.

The best thing is to order a
selection of *mezedes* and

FOOD AND DRINK

salads to share among you. The most interesting *mezedes* are *tzatziki* (yoghurt, garlic and cucumber dip); *melitzanosalata* (aubergine dip); courgettes or aubergines fried in batter; white haricot beans in vinaigrette sauce; *tiropitakia* or *spanakopites* (small cheese and spinach pies); *saganaki* (fried cheese); *oktapóth* (octopus); *mavromatika* (black-eyed peas); and *dolmadakia* (vine leaves stuffed with rice). Other typical *mezedes* are *garides* (shrimps), *feta* (white goat's cheese), *taramosalata* (pâté of smoked fish roe) and *bourekakia* (small meat pies).

Meat Dishes

Shish kebab (*souvlákia*) and chops (*brizoles*) are usually reliable choices. The best souvlaki is lamb (*arnisio*), but it is not often available. The small lamb cutlets called *paidhakia* are usually very tasty, as is roast lamb (*arni psito*) and roast kid (*katsiki*) when obtainable. *Kefthedes* (meatballs), *biftekia* (a type of hamburger), and the spicy sausages called *loukanika* are usually good and inexpensive, although minced meat is the most common source of stomach problems in Corfu as elsewhere, so care needs to be taken. Restaurants with a fast turnover, and frequented by locals, are likely to be safe. Outside the expensive restaurants and hotels, beef is difficult to find, is usually of inferior quality, and is invariably overpriced. Another meat-based main

course dish the visitor to Corfu is likely to encounter is *moussaka,* a pie made from aubergines, minced meat and potato topped with cheese sauce and baked.

Among the many other tasty main courses found in tavernas are *pastitsio* (macaroni with minced meat and bechamel sauce), *gemista* (either tomatoes or green peppers stuffed with meat or rice), *yiouvarelakia* (stewed meat balls with rice), *souzoukakia* (meat balls with tomato sauce and garlic), *stifado* (meat with onions), *kokoretsi* (skewer of liver and kidneys), and *pastitsada* (tomato stew).

Fish

Coastal tavernas in Corfu also offer fish and shellfish. *Kalamarákia* (fried baby squid) are widely available in summer, but the choicer fish, such as red mullet (*barboúnia*), and sea bream (*fangri*) are much less common and much more expensive.

Among the fish and seafood dishes fairly widely available are *astakós* (lobster), *kavouri* (crab), *stridia* (oysters), *midia* (clams), *lithrinia* (bass), *glossa* (sole), and *marides* (whitebait). *Youvetsi* is a shrimp casserole. Less pricey but equally tasty are *xifhias,* grilled pieces of swordfish served on skewers with onions, tomatoes and bay leaves. The price of fish is quoted by the kilo, and the standard procedure is to 'go to the glass' (which may mean a

FOOD AND DRINK

Fresh fish, fresh salads and a little ouzo are the ingredients for memorable meals on Corfu

tank or a refrigerator) and choose your own.

Desserts

Watermelons, melons and grapes are the standard summer fruit, and you will also find ice cream (*pagotó*), often home-made and usually creamy and delicious. Other desserts include *pastes* (very sweet cakes with cream), *baklavá* (syrup cake), *loukoumádes* (fritters with honey or syrup), and *kataifi* (shredded wheat soaked in honey).

Restaurants catering for tourists will serve desserts, but after a meal most Greeks prefer to go to a *zaharoplastion* (patisserie), where sticky, sweet confections are served with a glass of water, or may be taken out in a box.

Snacks

Traditional snacks are one of the delights of Greek cuisine, although they are being increasingly replaced by international favourites such as toasted sandwiches (*tost*) and pizzas. However, small kebabs (*souvlakia*) can sometimes be found in Corfu, especially in Corfu Town, and cheese pies (*tiropites*) can almost always be found at the baker's. Another popular snack is *yiro* (doner kebab), served in pita bread with garnish.

Drinks

Wine (*frasinos*) is commonly drunk on Corfu. White is *aspro krasi*, red is *mavro krasi*. *Retsina*, a wine flavoured with pine resin, which comes mainly from mainland Greece, should be served chilled and can come from bottles or from barrels. Greek brandy (*conyak*) can be excellent; cheaper brands tend to be rather sweet, while the well-known brands (usually more reliable) are Botrys, Metaxa and Cambas, of which different qualities are produced. Imported spirits and drinks such as whisky, gin and vermouth are more expensive than locally produced equivalents, many of which are acceptable for mixing.

Mandolata is a liquer made of strawberries and kumquats and comes in white or dark varieties. Beer (*bira*) in Corfu means lager, and the national brand, Fix, is considerably cheaper than the German and Dutch imports. Most tourist bars and tavernas are more likely to offer Amstel, Henninger, Heineken and Carlsberg. Soft drinks (*anapsiktika*) such as Coca Cola and Seven Up are widely available, but can be very expensive. It is often better to stick to mineral water – particularly the bottled spring water, which is superb. The Greek soft drinks tend to be very sweet and syrupy: *Portokalada* is a fizzy orange drink, and the cloudy-looking *lemonada* has a real taste of lemon. Few bars serve fresh orange juice, but you can buy this at mini-markets.

Instant coffee is widely available if the strong, thick and sweet Greek coffee is not to your liking, but specify when ordering. Coffee is taken on its own by most Greeks in a *kafeneion* (coffee-bar), particularly after a meal. Tea is not widely drunk, but is available in tourist areas, though seldom accompanied by milk.

SHOPPING

There are gift shops in most resorts, and a good range of shops in Corfu Town, which also has a colourful fruit and vegetable market every morning, just north of Platia Yeoryiou Theotoki, plus a fish market in the old town.

The National Organisation of Greek Handicrafts has a shop at 32 B X Stratigou Street, Corfu Town, offering a wide choice of Greek handicrafts, and a permanent display. Handicrafts are also sold at Danilia Village. Good buys

include leather goods, ceramics and jewellery. It is worth bargaining in the small souvenir shops when you are choosing gifts to take home. You will also see an array of handwoven and embroidered items such as doormats, carpets, tablecloths, napkins, aprons, skirts and blouses of lace and cotton. Particularly popular are cotton needlework shawls and bedspreads and

Handmade leather goods are a speciality, and visitors usually find that prices compare very favourably with those at home

heavy, white sweaters. Other Greek souvenirs worth considering include a strand of worry beads, typical Greek songs on cassette, skewers for souvlákia (some of which are very elaborate), and *brikia*, the long-stemmed Greek coffee pots. The area behind the Liston, around Áyios Spyridon and N. Theotoki Street, is a favourite place for souvenir-hunting. Although gold has a standard price worldwide, jewellery in Corfu Town is often less expensive than in many other places, even for 14, 18 and 21 carat gold, since tax is not added.

Leather goods are reasonably priced, and a wide range of bags, purses, wallets, shoes, sandals and belts is sold. Many ceramic items are made on the island by craftsmen, including copies of museum items.

Local craftsmen also carve bowls, trays and other household items from the island's olive wood.

Corfu honey, crystallised fruits, nougat and sugared nuts also make good gifts; the best choice is found in and around the fruit and vegetable market, to the north of Platia Yeoryiou Theotoki.

Shops in Corfu Town are open on Mondays, Wednesdays and Saturdays from 08.00 to 14.00 hours; and on Tuesdays, Thursdays and Fridays from 08.00 to 13.30 and again from 17.00 to 20.00. Other shops have similar hours, but not tourists' shops: see **Directory – Opening Times**.

ACCOMMODATION

Hotels in Corfu are classified according to the size of their rooms and public areas, the decor and furnishings of the rooms, and the service provided. 'Deluxe', 'A' and 'B' grade hotels have dining facilities on the premises; class 'C' does not.

Reservations at hotels can be made through a travel agent or the airline, by writing directly to the hotel or by contacting the Corfu Hotel Association, 12 Padara Street, Corfu (tel: 52233), or The Hellenic Chamber of Hotels, 24 Stadiou Street, Athens (tel: (01) 3236-962). There are also 'D' and 'E' class hotels, for which you should refer your enquiries to the island's Tourist Police.

Pensions

First-class pensions are listed by the National Tourist Organisation. Bedrooms are functional and usually without private facilities, and represent the most often found and reasonably priced accommodation on offer. Lists of lower-category pensions can only be obtained from the Tourist Police.

Rooms

A popular choice with independent travellers is to rent a room in a private house. Rooms are generally very clean, though with basic bathroom facilities. The option of a breakfast is sometimes made for a small additional charge. The Government-approved and categorised rooms are slightly more expensive than rooms in other households, but are of a reliable standard. Accommodation is seasonal, available mostly from May to September. Further information can be obtained from the Tourist Police who, along with local travel agents, can arrange bookings.

Self-Catering

An extensive range of self-catering properties (villas, apartments, bungalows and cottages) is offered by the Corfu Sun Club, 45-49 Arseniou Street, Corfu Town (tel: (0661) 33 855). A list of Campsites is given in the **Directory** of this book.

General Information

The standards of accommodation on the island, particularly in self-catering properties and pensions, are not comparable with those in other Mediterranean countries. Most tour operators try to ensure acceptable standards are maintained and that the accommodation offered is clean and comfortable, but 'luxuries' such as electric kettles, toasters, irons and a vast choice of kitchen utensils will almost certainly not be included in the equipment provided in self-catering apartments.

Many apartments and villas rely on solar heating systems; some have an electrical back-up system which is used only in bad weather. It is often necessary to contact the caretaker or owner if the weather is such that the electrical system needs to be used.

Apartments to let at Lakones, near Palaiokastrítsa – not all landscaping is as tactful as this

It has become standard practice for proprietors to ask to keep your passport, ostensibly 'for the Tourist Police' but in reality to prevent you leaving with an unpaid bill. Some owners may be satisfied with just taking down the details and they will almost always return the documents if you need them.

Water is a valuable commodity in Corfu, especially in the height of the summer, and visitors should expect an occasional drop in water pressure. An increasing number of properties rely on solar power to heat the water. In such cases, when the sun isn't shining, shortages of hot water have to be accepted.

ENTERTAINMENT AND NIGHTLIFE

Most of the principal resorts have discotheques aimed mainly at younger holidaymakers, especially Benitsai (Benitses). Most have a range of bars, from simple to lavish, with cocktail bars especially numerous (Dhasia is a good example). Those who fancy a flutter can try the Casino at the Akhillíon Palace. Folklore shows are staged frequently throughout the island. Versions of *Zorba the Greek* or *Sirtaki* dances can be seen in many tavernas in Corfu, where the waiters will be happy to teach you a few basic steps. But you will soon want to sit down and admire when the professional dancers take to the floor and give more elaborate performances, often including dancing in a ring of fire and lifting tables with their teeth. As a sign of appreciation, happiness and high spirits, the Greeks may start to smash their plates on the floor. Officially, plate smashing has been declared illegal as it was considered likely to encourage rioting, but it can be seen at nightclubs and restaurants with special licences that allow the smashing of unglazed pottery. Plate smashing can be a wonderful way of letting off steam – but don't get carried away, since you are charged for any plates you break! Brass band performances are given at the bandstand in Corfu Town on Sunday evenings in summer. The annual month-long Corfu Festival of the Arts takes place between September and October, with works by visiting companies of opera, classical music, ballet and theatre, taking place in the Municipal Theatre.

WEATHER AND WHEN TO GO

Although August is traditionally the most popular month to be in Corfu, when there can be a total of 360 hours of sunshine and the island is alive for 24 hours a day, the off-season months of spring, early summer and autumn are in many respects as attractive for a holiday here as the more crowded July, August and September.

In April and May, with the temperatures varying between 15 and 25°C (59 and 77°F), the island is at its most peaceful and uncrowded, and the countryside is carpeted with flowers. June, as the temperature rises into the upper 20s C (70s F) and lower 30s C (80s F) brings the first crops of fruit, including figs, and the first honey of the year. After the season is over, in October, the sea is still warm and it is not unusual to get perfect weather

Traditional dancing at the Corfu Festival in autumn

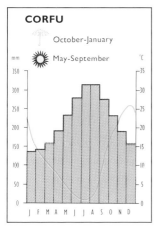

for much of the month –
although, since many hotels
close at the end of September,
the choice of accommodation
can be restricted.
Sea temperatures range from
an average of 16°C in April to
24°C in August, falling to 21°C
in October.

HOW TO BE A LOCAL

The Corfiots are a gentle,
friendly people who seldom
seem to get ruffled or
agitated, and who have a
tendency to sit back and take
things easy whenever the
opportunity arises. They will
linger for hours over a cup of
strong, Greek coffee
accompanied by a glass of
mineral water, chatting with
friends and watching the
world go by. A good place to
join them is at one of the
delightful cafés in the Liston,
that elegant arcade in the
Esplanade, in Corfu Town, or
better still at any pavement

café in the less developed
holiday resorts. The Corfiots
love food and eat out
regularly – though they avoid
the 'touristy' restaurants in
favour of simpler, less
sophisticated tavernas usually
found in side streets or alleys
– and this is where to search if
you're looking for genuine
local cuisine that is
reasonably priced.
For getting out and about, the
locals rely heavily on buses
which, though somewhat
erratic, are frequent and
cheap – unlike taxis and hire
cars – so if you want to do
some exploring, it makes
sense to follow their example.
Buses also let you see the
traditional, non-touristy side
of Corfu, as they potter
through remote villages.
Nudism is still against Greek
law, even though topless
sunbathing has become
accepted in most 'tourist'
resorts. Many people shed all
in isolated coves, ideally on
beaches accessible only by
private boat, and on the
beaches at Mirtiótissa and
Pélekas, where the local
police turn a blind eye. In
theory, though, should you
decide to strip, your action
could result in a fine or even
lead to a prison sentence.
Common sense should
dictate. The Corfiots are a
modest people, and visitors
should have regard for local
custom. It is considered bad
form for men or women to
wear shorts in churches or
museums. Women should
wear a scarf in church, no
matter how fleeting the visit.

PERSONAL PRIORITIES

Contraceptive pills are available, for tourists rather than the local population, but may not be found in the smaller resorts. The indigenous population still frowns on this – and on practically any other – form of birth control, and it is best to take your own supply with you. Condoms, however, are widely available.

Generally speaking, women should have little difficulty obtaining personal requisites such as tampons from larger pharmacies, but may have difficulty in small resorts. Female travellers run little risk of sexual harassment or intimidation when taking a holiday in Corfu. The small minority of Greeks who migrate to the resorts in summer in search of liberated tourists can sometimes be over-persistent in their advances, but on the whole the female visitor is more likely to be at risk from fellow holidaymakers than from the locals who live on the island.

CHILDREN

Corfu is a popular holiday destination for those with children, and is well equipped to cater for them. Many hotels have separate children's swimming pools, or areas of the main pool reserved for their use, and some of the larger establishments have children's play areas and offer children's menus and special programmes of games and activities.

Many of the island's beaches offer safe bathing, and are well equipped with watersports facilities. Some resorts have also installed water chutes which are particularly popular with youngsters.

At night most children are generally fascinated with the Greek evenings laid on at numerous tavernas and hotels throughout the island – and especially enjoy the opportunity for intentional plate smashing!

For children who prefer

Aeolos Beach Hotel, Pérama: sunbathing is a favourite pastime at this relaxed resort

burgers and fries to Greek food, Corfu surpasses most of its competitors, since the majority of restaurants and tavernas include precisely these dishes on their menus.

TIGHT BUDGET

As is the case with many holiday destinations, Corfu is cheapest in the low seasons. Many hotels, restaurants and sightseeing attractions on the island are closed during the winter months, so the best time to enjoy a holiday in Corfu – and save on expense – is in the spring and autumn, when hotel and holiday package rates are often less expensive than during the peak summer months of July and August. You can also cut the cost of a holiday in Corfu by opting for self-catering accommodation. The island offers a wide range of villas and apartments for holiday rental, most of them available through overseas tour operators, and these are invariably cheaper than hotels, especially if several adults are sharing. An inexpensive option for the lone traveller, or couple, is to stay in a pension or to rent a room in a private house (see **Accommodation**). Another tip is to avoid the well-developed resorts and choose instead one of the lesser known, off-the-beaten track places. Not only will you find these offer less expensive holiday accommodation, but prices in the restaurants and bars are usually lower than in the more popular, livelier resorts.

SPECIAL EVENTS

The biggest and most colourful celebrations in Corfu are religious festivals, and the most important is Greek Orthodox Easter (not always the same date as the Western Easter). Celebrations in the lead up to Easter begin in February with the Carnival, when for two weeks children in fancy dress run around the streets 'clubbing' each other with plastic batons, culminating on the final day of Mardi Gras (Shrove Tuesday) when there is a big parade in Corfu Town. Good Friday is a day of mourning throughout the island, and during the Saturday Midnight Mass (held in all churches) the 'light of resurrection' is passed by candle from one person to another. General jubilation commences, and continues on Easter Sunday with traditional lamb-roasting and dancing. Easter in Corfu, in fact, is very special – a mixture of East and West, of ecclesiastical, civic and military pomp, with a strongly individual flavour. The religious celebrations held in Corfu Town during Passion Week and on Easter Sunday are particularly splendid. The splendour of the occasion is heightened in the years when Easter in the Orthodox countries falls later than in the West, and the brilliant sunshine and fresh green of the trees give the ceremonies a natural framework of great beauty, complemented by the handsome Venetian and Georgian buildings of the town.

SPECIAL EVENTS

Bands are part of the St Spyridon processions four times a year

It all begins on Good Friday, when each church holds its solemn procession in memory of the burial of Christ. These processions go round the town until late evening, each of them watched by large crowds. On Holy Saturday there is another procession, but this time it is the town's miracle-working patron saint who is taken around the streets. St Spyridon, enshrined in his golden case, is borne upright so that his head, resting to one side, can be seen by the bystanders. At 11.00am the main streets are cleared by police and people take cover under the arcades, while from the upper storeys of houses descends a shower of pottery – old jugs, basins – anything that will smash into pieces – to the delight of the townsfolk and the bewilderment of visitors. No-one knows the exact origin of this custom, but a frequently given explanation is that it is a demonstration of anger at Judas's betrayal of Jesus. In the evening of Holy Saturday crowds again assemble and make their way to the Esplanade, for it is here, at midnight, that the Bishop announces the miracle of the Resurrection. At a quarter to midnight all is still, except for the subdued murmurings of the crowd. Then, slowly and in near darkness, the Bishop and clergy arrive in procession, followed by soldiers, sailors and civic officials. There ensues a short service after which, on the stroke of midnight, the band bursts into an Easter hymn, cannons roar from the fortress, fireworks scream into the air, bells in the town start ringing, and the place is once more bathed in light. Not only are hundreds of electric lights switched on, but everyone lights a candle.

Other Festivals

A procession of St Spyridon's body through the streets of Corfu Town takes place four times a year and is accompanied by bands. The processions are held on the following dates: on the Greek Orthodox Palm Sunday, on the morning of the following Saturday (as explained above for the Greek Easter), on 11 August, and on the first Sunday in November.
Another impressive religious celebration takes place on 14 August at Mandoúki, in honour of the Assumption of the Holy Virgin.
The fiesta at the village of Levkímmi, on 8 July, includes local dances.
May Day (1 May) is when everybody heads to the beach for a picnic – one of the best days for visiting empty towns.
Enosis Day (21 May) marks the day in 1864 when the island was handed from the British back to the Greeks, and is celebrated with a procession in Corfu Town.

SPORT

Corfiots are keen players of basketball and football, but for visitors there is a wide range of other sports to choose from, and much of the summer activity is, understandably, centred on sea and water sports.

Cricket

Cricket is played on the Esplanade, opposite the Liston. Two local clubs play here on Wednesday and Sunday afternoons in high summer, while, throughout September, a Cricket Festival features visiting teams. For details of matches contact the Corfu Cricket Technical Committee, 10 Alexandrias, Corfu (tel: 41526).

Fishing

There are excellent opportunities for fishing all over the island. No licence is needed, and it is easy to hire a boat and equipment.

Golf

The Corfu Golf Club has an 18-hole golf course in the Ropás Valley, surrounded by mountains and close to the lovely Ermónes bay. The 6,803-yard (6,220m) course has been praised as one of the finest in the Mediterranean, with a modern irrigation system keeping the turf in good condition even during times of drought. Amenities include a practice ground and a putting area as well as a clubhouse with an excellent restaurant and pleasant bar. A courtesy coach service also operates. Another course on the island is close to Ipsos.

SPORT

Gymnasium

The Corfu Gymnasium, near the Platitera Monastery on the Kondokáli road leading from Corfu Town, has all the latest body-building and exercise equipment.

Horseriding

The principal riding centres are Corfu Riding, Korkira Beach, Gouvía; Kerkira Golf Hotel (Corfu Town); and the Barrique Riding Stables in the tiny village of Afra, just north of Pélekas. There are also several pony trekking centres.

Squash

Courts are available at the Corcyra Beach Hotel, 5 miles (8km) outside Corfu Town at Gouvía, and visitors are welcome.

Tennis

If the hotel at which you are staying doesn't have tennis courts (and many do), there are two clubs with coaching available: the Corfu Tennis Club is in the centre of Corfu Town, at Romanou and Vraila Streets, and the other club is at Kefalomandouko, an area above the New Port Road, also in Corfu Town.

Ten-Pin Bowling

There is a bowling alley open to visitors at the Corfu Hilton situated just outside Corfu Town in Kanóni.

Walking

Inland Corfu seems little affected by tourism and offers fine walking country.
For suggestions of walking routes, *The Corfu Book of Walks* and *Landscapes of Corfu*, available from bookshops on the island, are invaluable.

Watersports

The sea round Corfu is warm and usually clear, with both sand and rocky coasts. The majority of the popular resorts offer a good range of sports, including paragliding, waterskiing, rowing and pedaloes. Some also hire out waterscooters and windsurfing equipment.
There is skindiving on both the east and west coasts – in fact, one diving school at Palaiokastrítsa was established over 25 years ago, and has been going strong ever since. Other schools for watersports are to be found in Dhasia, Kavos and Sidhári. At both the Baracuda Club at Palaiokastrítsa on the west coast and the Waterhoppers in Ipsos on the east coast, there's tuition for beginners and first-class equipment available.
For windsurfers, the best coast for picking up good winds is the west coast. The prevailing summer wind (usually in the afternoons) is a westerly. The east coast is generally calmer but offers good opportunities for beginners. Some windsurfing hire centres offer knowledgeable advice and a range of boards suitable for beginners and the more experienced – for instance at Áyios Yeóryios, near Límni Korríssia (Lake Korission), on the southwest coast.
For boat enthusiasts, there are sailing and yachting facilities in Corfu Town, Gouvía and Palaiokastrítsa.

DIRECTORY

Arriving

By Air

Although a few scheduled airlines operate direct, non-stop flights from European cities to Corfu, the majority of flights are routed via Athens, with an onward connection to Corfu. This latter section of the journey takes about 35 minutes.

In addition, numerous companies operate package holidays to Corfu incorporating a direct charter flight and accommodation in either hotels or self-catering villas or apartments.

The airport is situated just 1¼ miles (2km) to the south of Corfu Town. There is no public transport from the terminus building but buses to Corfu Town stop on the main road ¼ mile (500m) from the airport, while a courtesy bus service is operated by some hotels. Taxis also operate from the airport,

Autumn in Corfu Town: the crowds have gone, but the weather is still perfect

DIRECTORY

The point of arrival for passengers arriving by ferry

but agree a fare in advance or insist the driver uses the meter.

By Sea
There's an all year round car ferry service to Corfu from Brindisi, Italy. Various companies sail to Corfu including night crossings arriving in Corfu the following morning. Ferries also operate from the Italian ports of Ancona, Bari and Trieste, longer crossings but useful alternatives in high summer to busy Brindisi.

Corfu's main connection with the Greek mainland is the port of Igoumenitsa, with up to 20 sailings a day in high summer and eight in the winter (weather permitting); journey time about 1½ hours. A twice-daily service also operates from Saglada; a small town north of Igoumenitsa. Various sailings also leave from Patras on the Greek mainland.

By Road
Before the civil war and troubles in former Yugoslavia the usual route from Britain was from one of the Channel ports to either Ostend or Zeebruge, continuing on to Greece by way of Brussels, Cologne, Munich, Salzburg, Belgrade and Nis. From both eastern and northern Greece a road through Metsovo to Ioannina and then to Igoumenitsa, from where you could catch the local ferry to Corfu. Alternatively, motorists now travel through Italy, taking a car ferry directly to Corfu from one of the ferry ports, noteably Brindisi.

By Rail
The most popular route is via Paris and Berne to Italy, where ferries to Corfu can be joined at Brindisi or Ancona. Another

route is via Brussels, Munich, Belgrade and Athens. The journey time is about 2½ days. By road and train – in summer, car-sleeper trains operate from Boulogne, Brussels, Paris and 's-Hertogenbosch (Holland) to Milan, and on from Milan to connect with the ferry service to Corfu.

Entry Formalities

Passports but not visas are required for visitors from Western European countries (including British passport holders), Australia, New Zealand, Canada and the USA. A visa is not required for stays of up to three months in Greece (two months for USA and Portugal passport holders). If you want to stay longer than this period you should make an application. In Corfu, this can be done through the local police. It is advisable to do this a couple of weeks before your time runs out. Take your passport and keep your pink, personalised Bank exchange slips to prove you can support yourself without working. In return you will receive authorisation for a stay of up to six months.

Nationals of some other countries need visas, many do not; check before travelling.

Camping

Unauthorised camping is illegal, though the law is not always rigorously applied. Licenced sites operated by the Greek National Tourist Office have excellent facilities but can be expensive. Privately-run sites are more reasonable but generally have less in the way of amenities. An International Camping Carnet, though not normally requested, may result in a discount on your stay. For further details contact Association Greek Camping, 102 Solonos Street, 10680 Athens (tel: (01) 3621-560). The principal camping sites on Corfu are:

Dionysius Camping, opposite the bus stop at Komméno, is well-equipped with even a discotheque (tel: 91417).

Ippokambos (Sea Horse), Mesongí, PO Box 37 (tel: 25735/92864).

Karousádhes: on the beach of Karousádhes (tel: 31394).

Kerkyra Camping: on the beach at Ipsos (tel: 93246/93308/93579).

Kontokali Beach International: on the beach at Kondokáli (tel: 91202/91170).

Roda Beach: about half a mile (1km) from the beach at Ródha (tel: 93120/34761).

Chemist

See **Pharmacist**.

Crime

Crime is rare on Corfu, but it's still wise to take precautions such as depositing valuables in the hotel safe, if available, and taking care of your possessions when in public, especially on the beach or when shopping.

Customs

Foreign tourists may take into Corfu duty free:

If arriving from EC countries: 200 cigarettes **or** 50 cigars **or** 250 grams of tobacco; one litre of spirits **or** two litres of wines, sparkling wines or liqueurs;

50ml of perfume and 0.25 litres of toilet water.

If arriving from non EC countries: 200 cigarettes **or** 50 cigars **or** 250 grams of tobacco; one litre of spirits **or** four litres of wines, sparkling wines **or** liqueurs; 50ml of perfume and 0.25 litres of toilet water.

Visitors to Greece may, as a general rule, *temporarily* import personal articles duty-free, providing they are considered as being in use and in keeping with the personal status of the importer. Plants with soil are prohibited. Cats and dogs require health and rabies inoculation certificates issued by a veterinary authority in the country of origin not more than 12 months (cats six months) and not less than six days prior to arrival.

Importation of antiquities and works of art is free, but should be declared, together with their value, so that they may be freely exported. It is forbidden to export antiquities and works of art found in Greece. The duty-free allowance for goods *exported* from Greece will depend upon the traveller's nationality and the import regulations of the country of their destination, which should be consulted before departure.

Disabled

Little specific provision is made, but some accommodation is built with access needs in mind. The Greek National Tourist Organisation should have details of specialist travel companies if local travel agencies are unable to advise.

Once in Corfu, you should find the locals welcoming and helpful.

Driving

Renting a car or jeep is recommended for holidaymakers who want to do some exploring, especially if they are based in one of the more remote holiday resorts on the island.

There is no shortage of car hire firms, including well-known companies such as Avis and Hertz in Corfu Town, and local firms in all the major resorts. Prebooked and prepaid rates are normally cheaper than arranging hire when in Corfu. For driving on Corfu a valid pink EC licence, which includes translations, is acceptable. An International Driving Permit (IDP) is advisable for holders of other licences, such as the British green licence, because these do not carry translations. An IDP is compulsory for nationals of the USA, Canada and Australia. The IDP is best obtained from a motoring club at home.

A registration document and a green card of insurance are also required for temporarily imported vehicles.

To drive your own imported car or motorcycle over 50cc, the minimum age is 17, but you may have to be 23 years old to rent a vehicle, although many companies don't stick rigidly to this rule. Damage to tyres, wheels and the underside of cars is not normally covered by insurance.

Vehicles are driven on the right hand side of the road and,

unless otherwise indicated by signs, cars are subject to the following speed restrictions: 50kph (31mph) *in* built-up areas, 80kph (49mph) *outside* built-up areas, and 100kph (62mph) on dual-carriageways. Seat belts must be worn by law – though many hire cars aren't even fitted with them. It is also compulsory to carry a warning triangle, fire extinguisher and a first-aid kit – failure to comply may result in a fine.

Main roads are usually asphalted, but it is folly to drive at any speed. Curves are not usually signposted and are never banked, so great care is required. Secondary roads are sometimes very rough, and are often narrow, serpentine and steep. Animals frequently add to the risk – and the novelty – of driving in Corfu: goats, donkeys, sheep, chickens and gypsy carts may be encountered at any bend, even in the capital's suburbs.

Mopeds

Most travel companies do not advise their clients to hire mopeds because of the high risk element – most road casualties and fatalities in Corfu involve moped and scooter riders. However, if you decide to ignore the warnings, it's worth paying more for a reliable, quality machine – and it's equally important to take out full insurance. Above all, ride carefully and don't get carried away by the holiday atmosphere, and if possible wear a crash helmet. Most major resorts have moped hire firms.

Corfu Town has countless shops for souvenir hunting in its maze of narrow streets

Petrol

Petrol stations are open from 07.00 to 19.00 hours Monday to Saturday, and they operate a rota system to cover evenings until midnight, and Sundays. There is always a station open somewhere near Corfu Town, but out of town supplies are patchy.

Petrol (leaded) is sold as *Venzini Apli* (91-92 octane) and *Venzini Super* (96-98 octane). Unleaded petrol is sold as Super (95 octane) at stations displaying the sign. The acceptance of credit cards for petrol purchases is limited.

DIRECTORY

Electricity

The voltage in Corfu, as in the rest of Greece, is generally 220 volts AC. Plugs are of the common European round, two-pin type. Street lights are scarce in many parts of the island, so it's useful to take a torch with you, especially if you're staying in a villa or apartment that is off the beaten track.

Embassies and Consulates

British Consulate,
1 Menekratous Corfu Town.
Tel: 30055
Canadian Embassy,
Gennadiou 4, Ipsilantou 115–21, Athens. Tel: 723 9511
US Embassy, Vas Sofia 91, 115–21 Athens. Tel: 721 2951

Emergency Telephone Numbers

Ambulance 39403 (prefix with 0661 if calling from outside Corfu Town)

At its best Corfu can be very hard to beat

Coast Guard 32655
Emergency Road Assistance 104
Fire 199
First Aid 30562
International Telegram 155
Police 100
Rural Police Emergency 109

Entertainment Information

Your best bet is to refer to pages of the island's free-issue publication Corfu News, published monthly (see **Media** for details).

Entry Formalities

See **Arriving**.

Health

There are no required inoculations for Corfu, or other parts of Greece, but it's a sensible precaution to have a typhoid-cholera booster and to ensure that you are up-to-date on tetanus and polio. British (upon production of Department of Health form E111) and other EC nationals are entitled to free medical care, but this means admittance

only to the lowest grade of hospital, and does not include nursing care. In any case, treatment and prescribed medicines are first paid for, and the costs are then refunded by the Greek authorities. If you require prolonged medical care or are from a country outside the EC you'll need to make use of private treatment, which is expensive, so travel insurance, with cover for private medical treatment, is essential.

The water is considered quite safe to drink, but most visitors prefer to avoid tap water and ice and use bottled water even to brush their teeth. There are pharmacies in the major resorts if sickness or diahorrea does occur, but it's worth taking a small medical kit including aspirins, plasters and a branded product of your choice for stomach upsets. Sunburn can also be a major health problem, so use a good prevention cream and go for a steady tan; remember, even when the breeze blows you can still burn.

The main hospital, at Ioulias Andreadi Street, Corfu Town (near Platia Yeoryiou Theotoki), has a 24-hour casualty department, at which English is spoken (tel: 30562 and 30033).

Most doctors pride themselves on their English. Look out for the sign IATPEION which indicates a doctor's clinic or surgery.

Holidays

On the following public and religious holidays all beaches and most shops close; they also close the afternoon before and the morning after a religious holiday. If a national holiday falls on a Sunday, it is the following Monday which is observed. Note that the Greek Orthodox Easter can fall several weeks before or after the Western Easter.

New Year's Day, Epiphany (6 January), Independence Day (25 March), Good Friday, Easter Sunday and Monday (March/April), Labour Day (1 May), Ionian Day (21 May), Whit Monday (May/June), Assumption Day (15 August), Holy Cross Day (14 September), National Holiday – Óchi day (28 October), Christmas and Boxing Day.

Lost Property

If you lose anything on the island try calling the Lost and Found Office (tel: (0661)39294), or the Office at the airport (tel: (0661)33576). Greek people have a reputation for honesty, and the Corfiots are no exception. For property lost in your hotel, report to the management or travel representative. For articles lost elsewhere, contact the tourist police.

Media
Television

There are a number of television channels in Greece including ET1 and ET2. All channels carry numerous English-language programmes and films.

Radio

Some Greek radio stations sometimes have programmes

of interest to the foreign listener. ERT (1st programme), located at 1008 KHz and 297.6 m or 91.80 MHz, presents the news in English daily at around 07.40, preceded by a weather forecast and sea conditions programme at 06.30. ERT 2, on 981 KHz and 305.8 m, has two newscasts daily in English and French, going out at around 14.20 and 21.20. To receive the BBC World Service, tunc to the 49 metres band on short wave; in the evening, try medium wave.

Newspapers

Overseas newspapers are available around a day after publication; and in addition, the *Athens News* is published daily and is in English. The most informative newspaper for English-speaking visitors, however, is the free-issue, monthly *Corfu News*. Available from offices of the Greek National Tourist Organisation, the publication includes topical articles relating to the island plus a mine of extremely useful information on bus and ferry-boat travel, entertainment and nightlife, dining, museums and places of interest, sports and lists of doctors, dentists and chemists.

Money Matters

Greek currency is the drachma. The most common notes in circulation are those of 50, 100, 500, 1,000, and 5,000 drachmas, and coins 5, 10, 20, 50 and 100 drs.
You are officially allowed to take up to a maximum of 100,000 drachma notes into Corfu. Upon your return, no more than 20,000 drachma may be taken out of Greece. There are no restrictions on the import or export of foreign currency up to the equivalent of $1,000, but amounts in excess of this must be declared to the Currency Control Authorities on arrival. Most visitors take their money in the form of travellers' cheques, but a small amount of local currency is worth acquiring in advance, especially if arriving at weekends when banks and some currency exchange offices will be closed. Travellers' cheques can be cashed at all banks, and at numerous hotels, agencies and tourist shops. Take your passport with you, as it will normally be required in any exchange.
Eurocheques are widely accepted at banks and can be written out in drachmas. Commission on travellers' cheques is paid when you buy them and also to the exchanging bank. With most Eurocheques you pay a commissioning charge of around 1.6 per cent to the exchanging bank plus a handling fee per transaction. Most major credit cards are fairly widely accepted in the larger resorts, but only by the more expensive shops, hotels and restaurants. They are particularly useful for large purchases, like hiring cars, but are no use in tavernas.
The only banks on the island are in Corfu Town, and these

are open from 08.00 to 14.00 Monday to Friday. Take your passport and be prepared to queue. There is also a limited number of authorised exchange bureaux in the larger resorts, which may open in the afternoon, while most good hotels will accept foreign currency and travellers' cheques, at a poorer rate.

The island's main post office, in Corfu Town on Alexandras Avenue, has facilities for currency exchange, including cashing travellers' cheques and Eurocheques. With commission rates at up to half that of banks, it is worth bearing in mind when changing large sums of money.

Some branches of banks now have automatic teller machines which operate 24 hours a day and will take the appropriate cashcard.

Opening Times
Shops
Shops are generally open from 08.00 to 13.30 and again from 17.00 to 20.00 on Tuesday, Thursday and Friday but from 08.00 to 14.00 only on Monday, Wednesday and Saturday. Supermarkets out of town are open all day until late. Tourist shops, too, are usually open into the evening.

Museums
Museums on the island have no standard times, but generally are closed on Mondays or Tuesdays, while Sundays and holidays sometimes mean free admission.

'Wounded Achilles' is one of many statues in the gardens of the Akhillíon Palace, Corfu Town

For opening times of post offices and pharmacists, see separate entries in this directory (for bank opening times see under **Money Matters** opposite).

Personal Safety
Watch out for the lethal three-sided lifts fitted in many hotels in Corfu. These lifts have no inner door, so as they move passengers run the risk of abrasion or worse against the wall. A few lifts carry signs warning children not to use the lift without an adult present, but it's advisable to take extra care.

The hot climate of Corfu is, as one would expect, the kind that attracts reptiles, insects – mosquitoes included – and a

variety of other animal life.
These are harmless, although
mosquitoes are often a real
nuisance. The most effective
way to deter them is by using
tablets with electrical hotplates.
You simply plug them in
overnight in a ventilated area,
away from draughts. They can
be bought locally for around
1,000 drachmas; one trade
name is *Doker Mat*.
Alternatively, coils which you
leave to smoulder like incense
sticks, as well as sprays, are
also available. Sprays are best
applied just before dark, with
the windows closed for a while.

Pharmacist
Pharmacies, or chemists,
provide the normal remedies
and are happy to give advice
on minor ailments. Most items
are available without a
prescription, although
medicines are not particularly
cheap.
Pharmacies are open during
normal shopping hours, except
on Saturdays, and are also
closed on Sundays. Outside
these hours a 24-hour rota
system operates, the list being
displayed in each shop (in
Greek) and in the *Corfu Sun*
newspaper (in English).

Places of Worship
Roman Catholic
Church next to the Town Hall in
Corfu Town. Services
June–September daily at 08.00,
and October–May 08.30.
Sunday and holiday masses at
07.30, 08.30, 10.00 and 19.00

Anglican
Church at Mavali 21, next to the
old Parliament Building in

*Vatonies, near Palaiokastrítsa:
inland Corfu is worth exploring*

Corfu Town. Services are held
on Sundays at 10.30.

Jewish Synagogue
Paleologou Street, Corfu Town.

Police
The special Tourist Police
(Touristiki Astinoma) on duty in
Corfu Town and in resorts, can
assist tourists by offering
information on the island, even
helping to find accommodation.
They can be distinguished from

Alexandras Avenue in Corfu Town. It is open from 07.30 to 20.00 hours Monday to Friday, and 07.30 to 14.00 on Saturday and on Sunday from 09.00 to 13.30.

Stamps may also be bought from kiosks or from shops selling postcards. Post boxes are painted yellow.

Air mail letters take three to six days to reach the rest of Europe, five to eight days to reach North America, and a little longer to Australia and New Zealand. Postcards can be very slow indeed: up to two weeks for Europe, and up to a month to North America or the Pacific.

A modest fee for express service cuts letter delivery time to about two days for Europe and three days for North America.

Public Transport
Buses

Corfu Town is the centre of public transport, and buses from here go all over the island, which is well served by roads. In general, green and white buses leave the bus station at New Fortress Square for the resorts and outlying areas, while blue buses serve Corfu Town, its suburbs (Mandoúki and Kanóni) and local villages and leave from stations at Platia Yeoryiou Theotoki and the Esplanade. Suburban services circle the town, with no terminal. The best places to pick them up in the town centre are close to Platia Yeoryiou Theotoki or in the Esplanade. The island's bus service is reasonably priced, but the

other policemen by little flags worn on their pockets, showing which language(s) they speak. Their main office is in Corfu Town in the Palace of St Michael and St George (the same building as the tourist office; tel: 30265). They are available daily from 07.00 to 22.00.

Post Office

Many of the island's resorts have mobile post vans which can be recognised by a yellow sign reading OTE. Apart from these, the main post office is on services are staggered, often unreliable, and become very overcrowded at times. Before 15 June and after 15 September there is a reduced service.

Boats
Boats leave from below the Esplanade, Corfu Town, for places on the coast north of Corfu Town as far as Kassiópi, and on the south coast down to Kavos.
The small islands of Erikoúsa, Mathráki and Othonoí (to the north of Corfu), have a twice-weekly service.

Boats moored at sunset in Garítsa Bay, with the Old Fortress in Corfu Town beyond

Connections with the Greek mainland (Igoumenitsa) and the island of Paxoí are served by the Old Port to the east of the New Fortress, while inter-island ferry services call at the New Port, Xenofondos Stratigou.

For sailing schedules you should contact the Port Authority or the National Tourist Office in Corfu Town.

Taxis
Taxis are either tan or blue with a taxi sign on top and are usually Mercedes. They can be flagged down in the street, but in outlying areas it is best to call 'radio taxi' (tel: 33812). Most now have meters so there's no dispute over the fare; otherwise agree a price with the driver before getting in.

Senior Citizens
Corfu is not a holiday destination that springs to mind in this respect, but outside the hustle and bustle of the main holiday season, when the weather is more temperate, there is the natural beauty of the island for older visitors to enjoy. They would be well advised to avoid the bigger, longer-established resorts however. Many travel companies offer attractive rates to senior citizens booking a holiday of several weeks.

Student and Youth Travel
Students of any age should obtain an International Student Identity Card, ensuring discounts, not only in respect of travel, but also in entry to museums, archaeological sites and some forms of entertainment on Corfu.

Those under 26 years of age, but not a student, may consider applying for membership of The Federation of International Youth Travel Organisation, which guarantees discounts from several ferry and tour operators.

Youth Hostel
There is one official youth hostel on the island, located at Kondokáli (tel: 91292), four miles (7km) from Corfu Town.

Telephones
Local calls can be made at newspaper kiosks in Corfu Town or from coffee bars in resort areas. The island's telephone codes are 0661 (Corfu Town and surrounding areas), 0662 (south), and 0663 (north). Calls abroad are best made from the main post office (OTE) situated at 9 Mantzarou Street, Corfu Town (just off Platia Yeoryiou Theotoki). It is open 07.00 to 23.00 daily. There's another OTE office behind the Liston at 78 Kapodistriou Street.
Both these exchanges use a meter system, where the time is calculated in units. At the end of the call you pay for the number of units used.
An increasing number of restaurants and tavernas have metered telephones from which overseas calls can be made. It is also possible to make international calls from telephone kiosks using a phone card which can be purchased from OTE or newsagents.
To dial abroad, dial the international country code and the telephone area code (omitting the initial '0'), followed by the number.

International Dialling Codes from Corfu:
United Kingdom   00 44
Eire   00 353
USA and Canada   00 1
Australia   00 61
Dial 161 for international telephone information.
To call from overseas, use the international code for Greece, then one of the three island codes, omitting the initial '0'.

Useful Numbers
(see also **Emergency Telephone Numbers**)
Telephone Information 131. Use prefix 0661 for calls from outside Corfu Town area.
Tourist Information (EOT) 37638, 37640, 37639
Tourist Police 30265
Aliens Bureau 39494
Corfu Town Traffic Police 22353
Rural Traffic Police 30669
Port Police 32655
Passport Control 38088
Corfu Town Hall 39553
Prefect Office 36972
Post Office 39265/25544
International Shipping Information 32655
Port Authority 30481
Ferries: Greece-Italy 30481
Ferries: Corfu-Igoumenitsa 32655
Airport 30180
Olympic Airways 38695
Bus Terminal (Corfu Town) 30627
Bus Terminal (for Athens) 39985
Radio Taxi 33811/2
Archaeological Museum 30680
Palace Museum 30443
Cathedral 37007
Áyios Spyrídon 33059
Monastery of Platitera 37839

DIRECTORY

Time

Greek time is two hours ahead of Greenwich Mean Time and British Summer Time, except for short periods in the spring and autumn, when Greek clocks are changed in advance of British clocks. Local time is seven hours ahead of US and Canada, Eastern Time, and eight hours behind Australian New South Wales Time.

Tipping

By law, service charges are included in the bills at hotels, restaurants and tavernas. The Corfiots aren't tip-crazy, but they do expect you to leave a little something extra if they've given good service. In general, 10 per cent is a satisfactory amount to leave as a tip.

Toilets

Greek plumbing leaves a lot to be desired. The ancient Greeks may have been the pioneers of civilisation, but the new generation are certainly low down the list in the plumbing league… although, to be fair, things have considerably improved in recent years. However, with the influx of tourists, some anomalies in the plumbing systems are bound to occur throughout the season, especially during July and August. Small hotels and pension-type places request guests to place used toilet paper in a pedal bin. The reason is that the pipes are narrow, so if you don't follow the instructions you block the lavatory.

Tourist Offices

The Greek National Tourist Organisation (GNTO) maintains offices in:-
Australia and New Zealand: 51-57 Pitt Street, Sydney, NSW 2000 (tel: 241 1663/4).
Canada: 1233 Rue de la Montagne, Montreal, Quebec H3G 1Z2 (tel: 871 1532); and 68 Scollars Street, Toronto, Ontario, Lower Level, Unit E, M5R 1G2 (tel: 9682 220).
UK and Eire: 195/197 Regent Street, London W 1R 8DL (tel: 071 734 5997).
US: 645 Fifth Avenue, Olympic Tower, New York, NY 10022 (tel: 212 421 5777); 611 West Sixth Street, Suite 1998, Los Angeles, California 90017 (tel: 213 626 6696); and 168 North Michigan Avenue, Chicago, Illinois 60601 (tel: 312 782 1084).
On Corfu the National Tourist Organisation (EOT) provides useful, free brochures, maps, timetables and programmes of events. Its main office is open 07.30 to 14.30 daily, except Sunday, and is found in the centre of the capital, Corfu Town, at 15 K. Zavitslanou Street New Fortress), PO Box 245, 49100 Corfu (tel: 37638, 37640, 37639).

Travel Agencies

There are a number of travel agencies strung out along Arseniou, Kapodistriou and Xenofontos Stratigou Streets in Corfu Town. One of the most helpful is **Charitos Travel** at 35 Arseniou Parade (tel: 36825/6) offering excursions, boat trips, as well as car and scooter hire. Another reliable agency is **Greek Skies** at 20A Kapodistriou Street (tel: 39160).

LANGUAGE

Unless you know the Greek
script, a vocabulary is not of
very much use to the visitor. But
it is helpful to know the
alphabet, so that you can find
your way around, and the
following few basic words and
phrases will help too. (See also
Food and Drink page 97).

Alphabet

Alpha	Αα	short a, as in hat
Beta	Ββ	v sound
Gamma	Γγ	guttural g sound
Delta	Δδ	hard th, as in father
Epsilon	Εε	short e
Zita	Ζζ	z sound
Eta	Ηη	long e, as in feet
Theta	Θθ	soft th, as in think
Iota	Ιι	short i, as in hit
Kappa	Κκ	k sound
Lambda	Λλ	l sound
Mu	Μμ	m sound
Nu	Νν	n sound

Xi	Ξξ	x or ks sound
Omicron	Οο	short o, as in pot
Pi	Ππ	p sound
Rho	Ρρ	r sound
Sigma	Σσ	s sound
Taf	Ττ	t sound
Ipsilon	Υυ	another ee sound, or y as in funny
Phi	Φφ	f sound
Chi	Χχ	guttural ch, as in loch
Psi	Ψψ	ps, as in chops
Omega	Ωω	long o, as in bone

Beach tavern at Glifádha

Numbers

1	éna	14	dekatéssera
2	dío	15	dekapénde
3	tría	16	dekaéxi
4	téssera	17	dekaeptá
5	pénde	18	dekaokto
6	éxi	19	dekaennía
7	eptá	20	íkosi
8	októ	30	triánda
9	ennía	40	saránda
10	déka	50	penínda
11	éndeka	100	ekató
12	dódeka	101	ekaton éna
13	dekatría	1000	chília

LANGUAGE

Basic Vocabulary

good morning	kaliméra
good evening	kalispéra
goodnight	kaliníkta
goodbye	chérete
hello	yásou
thank you	efcharistó
please/you're welcome	parakaló
yes	ne
no	óchi
where is...?	poo íne?
how much is...?	póso káni?
I would like	tha íthela
do you speak English?	milate angliká?
I don't speak Greek	then miló hellinká

Places

street	ódos
avenue	léofóros
square	platía
restaurant	estiatório
hotel	xenodochío
room	domátio
post office	tachithromío
letter	grámma
stamps	grammatóssima
police	astinomía
customs	teloniakos
passport	diavatirion
pharmacy	farmakio
doctor	iatrós
dentist	odontiatros
entrance	isothos
exit	éxothos
bank	trápeza
church	eklisía
hospital	nosokomío
café	kafeneion

Travelling

car	aftokínito
bus	leoforío
train	tréno
boat	karávi
garage	garaz
train station	stathmos
bus station	stasi ton leoforio

airport	aerodromio
ticket	isitirio

Food

food	fagitó
bread	psomi
water	neró
wine	krasí
beer	bira
coffee	kafé

Fish

lobster	astakós
squid	kalamarákia
octopus	oktapóthi
red mullet	barboúnia
whitebait	marídes
sea bream	sinagritha

Meat/Poultry

lamb	arnáki
chicken	kotópoulo
meat balls	kefthedes
meat on a skewer	souvlákia
liver	skíti

Vegetables

spinach	spanáki
courgette	kolokithia
beans	fasolia

Salads and Starters

olives	eliés
yoghurt and cucumber dip	tzatziki
tomato and cucumber salad	angour domata
stuffed vine leaves	dolmadakia
'Greek' salad with cheese	horiatiki

Desserts

honeycake	baklavá
honey puffs	loukoumádes
semolina cake	halvá
ice cream	pagotó
yoghurt	yiaourti
shredded wheat and honey	kataifi
custard tart	bougatsa

INDEX

INDEX/ACKNOWLEDGEMENTS

The Automobile Association would like to thank the following photographers and libraries for their assistance in the preparation of this book:

MARTIN TRELAWNY took all the photographs in this book except those listed below. (© AA Photo Library)

J ALLAN CASH PHOTO LIBRARY 9 Corfu Town, 60 Vlakhérna Convent, 63 Kavos Coast, 108 Procession.

J CADY 5 Olive Trees, 35 Near near Aríllas, 37 Ayios Stéfanos, 116 House.

NATURE PHOTOGRAPHERS LTD 83 British Cemetery (R Bush), 84 Blue Rock Thrush (M Gore), 85 Shrike (P R Sterry), 87 Dappled White Butterfly (K J Carlson), 88/9 Petalia, Pandokrátor (R Bush), 91 Pond Terrapin, 92 Swallowtail Butterfly (S C Bisserot), 93 Roller (K J Carlson), 95 Corfu in April (R Bush), 96 Reinhold's Orchid (D M Turner Ettinger).

SPECTRUM COLOUR LIBRARY Cover: Pondikonísi, 40/1 Barmbáti, 64/5 Kondokáli Beach, 77 Sidhari, 78/9 View, 80 Paxoí.

Authors Acknowledgement
The author is indebted to Hogg Robinson Travel for permission to make use of regularly updated information on holiday resorts and hotels in Corfu.

For this revision: copy editor Jenny Fry; verifier: Mick Rebane
Thanks also to Gerry Crawshaw for his help with this revision.